STARTING AND RUNNING A NURSERY
The Business of Early Years Care

Helen Jameson • Madeline Watson

Stanley Thornes (Publishers) Ltd

First published in 1998 by:
Stanley Thornes (Publishers) Ltd
Ellenborough House
Wellington Street
Cheltenham
GL50 1YW
UK

A catalogue record for this book is available from the British Library.

ISBN 0-7487-3347-7

98 99 00 01 02 / 10 9 8 7 6 5 4 3 2 1

Typeset by Columns Design Ltd, Reading
Printed and bound in Great Britain by Redwood Books Ltd., Trowbridge

CONTENTS

BIOGRAPHICAL DETAILS

Helen Jameson MA ACA MIMC has a thorough grounding in business and financial management through her training as a chartered accountant and her subsequent experience of banking and management consultancy, in each case with major international organisations. She has worked with a diverse range of private and public sector organisations. As a management consultant she advises clients on key business management issues and is involved with practice development and technical training. She has applied her business and financial disciplines and experience to the on-going development of good practice in the general management of nursery provision. She is a working mother with two young children.

Madeline Watson MEd MIPD FRSA is a childcare provider, a qualified teacher and an OFSTED RGNI Inspector who, for 20 years, has specialised in managing community-based early years services. Her expertise touches on health as well as employment and early years issues. She has been actively involved in influencing policy and practice through participation in a number of national voluntary organisations. She has also maintained a parallel involvement with a range of local initiatives in London. Madeline's practice-based skills and knowledge underpin her consultancy work with local government and private sector employers. Her professional life is governed by a holistic approach to services for young children.

INTRODUCTION

A ringing telephone during the working day has frequently signalled contact from someone seeking friendly help and advice about nursery management – usually as a small business. Many of the individuals who contact us have areas of expertise, either in childcare, education or business, but recognise that they still need some help.

This book is intended to bridge the knowledge gaps, and to steer providers of early years service in the right direction. It is our intention to provide a realistic review of what is involved in operating a nursery in order to save those considering nursery management time and money, and to prevent worry or discouragement. We want to lend support to ambitions and to increase confidence, but also to advise caution, patience and realism.

Throughout the book we have placed a strong emphasis on good practice. This is especially significant in terms of the service offered to the children and their parents. It must never be forgotten that the child's best interests are paramount, and that nursery providers are taking on a duty of care for each child enrolled.

This book is structured to provide an overview of the key factors and the legal obligations involved in operating a nursery. The complexity of the responsibilities involved is stressed and sources of further in-depth guidance are suggested. A checklist is provided for each chapter to facilitate action and to act as an *aide-mémoire*.

We suggest that providers read through the whole of the book first before embarking on any one activity, because the subjects of various chapters are interrelated in many respects. One factor should not be considered without the other. There is a strong interplay between the financial, business, childcare and employment elements. Budgets must strike a good balance between all the competing demands, but should put the greatest emphasis on factors which affect the quality of care, such as staffing and safety.

This book does not attempt to provide specific answers to everything. Instead it is anticipated that readers will be cued to identify critical factors, and then to look at a variety of models to find out what is 'right' for their particular circumstances.

We have made no recommendations about budgets, staff pay or levels of fees. These should begin to emerge from the early planning work and information about current local conditions and childcare provision.

Finally, it must be acknowledged that this book owes much to our courageous clients who have shared their questions and have provided us with opportunities to observe and advise. We also wish to record our particular appreciation for past and future dialogues with professional colleagues. A number of people and organisations have helped us to frame the issues. Comments on the first draft were generously offered by Susan Brown, Jane Lane, Sue Owen, Helen Penn, Barbara Herts and Chris Howson. We have also gained much insight from Louise Hodgson and Lesley Richardson. We hope that our contribution in the form of this book will encourage new developments and good practice which will be of benefit to young children.

Helen Jameson and Madeline Watson

PART A
Getting Started

This section is about planning and preparation. Together the chapters cover the main things you will need to think about and do before you embark on definitive plans to open your nursery – and in particular before you invest in premises and begin recruiting a nursery team.

To a large extent the chapters are business oriented, reflecting the importance of proper planning and research at the commencement of any business venture. Nevertheless your plans will need to encompass your vision of your nursery, and it would be unwise to develop your business plan without reference to the child-care management practices and quality standards covered in later sections.

Finding suitable premises and adapting them as a nursery is one of the most difficult steps in starting a nursery, and can prove to be a major obstacle. This section includes chapters which suggest how to set about finding premises, and some of the design considerations for your nursery space.

1 MARKET RESEARCH

What this chapter covers:
- **The value of market research**
- **Establishing trends in childcare**
- **Conducting local market research**
- **Preparing a market research report**

The best preparation for tomorrow is to do today's work superbly well.
Sir William Osler

In this chapter we emphasise the importance of thorough market research as the basis of your plans for your nursery. We describe the main components of a market research report, and how this document links to other planning documents that you will need to prepare. This chapter is about asking questions – lots of them – and how to set about answering them so that you can make an informed decision about whether and how to proceed with your nursery.

The value of market research

When you decide to look seriously at starting a nursery, you may be convinced that the venture cannot possibly fail. You may have been trying to find a good nursery for your own child, or have spoken to many other parents who are finding it difficult to register their child with a good nursery. You may be working with a large or small business which has been trying to help staff find and arrange suitable childcare, or you may have read press or research reports which highlight the shortage of nursery provision in the UK. Assimilating all of this information will have brought you to the point of wanting to investigate the feasibility of setting up a nursery. At this stage it is essential that you formalise your market research before embarking on your plans, and before making any major financial commitment to your planned nursery.

WHY CONDUCT MARKET RESEARCH?

Nurseries require a significant investment if they are to be successful.
- Capital is needed to buy or rent premises, adapt them for use as a nursery, furnish and equip them, and make them safe for children.
- Additional finance is needed to cover any cash deficits during the first year of opening, e.g. to pay a core team of staff when the nursery first opens and there are few children in the nursery.

The finance for the nursery may come from a range of sources such as:

- bank loans
- venture capital
- your own savings
- a family member or a friend
- a local employer
- grant funding.

Whatever the source of funding, the people providing it will wish to be sure that the business has the best chance of success by meeting a genuine local need. Market research will help you to demonstrate this.

Market research will also help you refine what is known in business terms as your service offering. This is the total package of services you will be offering your customers. Your customers may be:

- individual parents
- a local employer using the nursery
- the local authority buying places in the nursery
- a training course buying places for students
- other groups of users.

The service offering includes:

- the ages of children for whom your nursery will cater
- the opening hours and days
- the childcare philosophy you will adopt
- the type of programme you will run for children
- whether or not you will offer part-time, sessional or emergency places as well as full-time places.

It is important to define your customers, to find out what services will meet their needs, to determine whether and how you will offer these, and to find out how much customers are willing to pay for these services.

Wherever you operate you will have competitors. These may include other nurseries, whether private, state or voluntary sector, childminders, playgroups and nannies. It is important to understand:

- who these competitors are
- what they offer
- how you will differentiate your services from theirs.

Your market research will enable you to do this. Without an awareness of competitors and their strategies, you may find that you are unable to attract parents to your nursery.

Market research will also help you determine what fees to charge. How to set fees is discussed in more detail in the Chapter 3, but the information that you obtain through your market research will be invaluable in judging the level at which to set fees.

WHERE TO START

In your market research you should look at the general social, economic and other trends which are influencing the demand for and supply of childcare

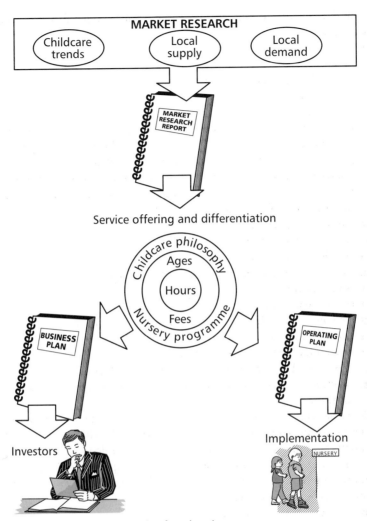

MARKET RESEARCH

Childcare trends | Local supply | Local demand

MARKET RESEARCH REPORT

Service offering and differentiation

Childcare philosophy · Ages · Hours · Fees · Nursery programme

BUSINESS PLAN

OPERATING PLAN

Investors

Implementation

Market research as the starting point for planning

generally, and of nursery places specifically. You will also need to find out what local factors are affecting the demand for and supply of nursery places in the specific area in which you are planning to locate your nursery. Both aspects of your research are important, especially to support the case you present to an outside investor, but your time and effort should be concentrated mainly on your local research. Nurseries tend to have relatively narrow catchment areas, so that they each operate in a very specific local market.

WATCH POINT

Given the difficulty of finding suitable premises for a nursery, it can be useful to carry out an initial assessment of several possible areas, to identify those in which to concentrate a premises search. In this initial assessment you will be assessing the economic prosperity of an area, and whether there is likely to be unmet demand for nursery places.

Establishing trends in childcare

The purpose of looking at overall trends in childcare is to ascertain the prospects for the childcare services sector as a whole. Any information you can provide on national trends will help your case with an outside investor, especially with the use of quotations from the quite numerous reports which have been published on the development of childcare in the UK.

QUESTIONS TO ASK

Typically research into childcare trends addresses the following questions:
- What are the demographic (population) trends?
- Will there be more or fewer under-fives in the next five to ten years (i.e. will your customer base be growing or shrinking)?
- What are the employment trends, especially among mothers?
- Do more mothers want to work?
- Can these mothers find good childcare?
- What does research demonstrate about the benefits of pre-school education?
- Are parents becoming more aware of the benefits?
- What is the Government policy with regard to childcare?
- Is the Government planning to provide state places for all?
- Is the Government looking for partnerships with the private sector?
- Will state pre-school education meet the needs of working parents?
- Is tax relief, grants, vouchers or some other form of subsidy for childcare on the agenda, hence making childcare affordable for more people?
- What are the opposition parties' policies on these issues?
- What childcare provision is available for under-fives in the UK?
- What percentage of the under-fives population has access to full-time nursery places?
- What percentage of under-twos has access to nursery places?
- Are there any large childcare companies who operate nationally and who might pose a competitive threat?
- Who are these companies?
- What services do they offer?
- How do they differentiate themselves?

WHERE TO FIND THE ANSWERS

A number of reports have been written on the availability and development of childcare in the UK, and these provide much of the information needed. New research is published each year, and old studies soon become out of date, so you will need to find the most up-to-date studies available at the time of conducting your research.

Research institutes which have published research on childcare include:

- The Adam Smith Institute
- The National Economic Development Office.

Other Government publications which provide information on population and related trends include:

- General Household Surveys
- Labour Force Surveys.

Conducting local market research

The success of a nursery depends largely on establishing a good local reputation, and making contact with and becoming part of the local community. Local market research is the first step in this process, and will help you lay the groundwork for a good network of local contacts. Treat it as a period of making friends as much as a time for pure information gathering.

ASSESSING DEMAND

A key purpose of your local research is to gauge the expected demand for nursery places. Will there be enough families looking for childcare, and who will be interested in using a nursery rather than any other form of childcare? Questions to ask typically include:

- Is there a large under-five population in the area?
- Is this expected to grow or decline?
- What are the local unemployment rates?
- Are these rates high or low?
- Is anything expected to change these, e.g. any local regeneration initiatives?
- Are there a large number of working parents?
- Or is this an area where few mothers work?
- Would the families where the mother is at home still wish to use a nursery for pre-school experiences, and do they have disposable income to pay for this?
- Where do local people work? Do they work locally or do they travel outside the area to work? This might influence whether they would look for nursery places near to home or to work, and the opening hours they would need.
- Is the area generally prosperous?
- Would you expect parents to be able to afford nursery provision?
- Is there a large local employer who might be interested in purchasing places in your nursery?
- Is there a large in-bound working population? There may be people coming to the area every day who would look for childcare near their place of work.
- Is there a local culture of using nurseries? In some areas parents tend to use childminders, and in others they use nannies. This can be a barrier to parents

looking at other forms of childcare, when their peer group are all using other childcarers.

- Is there a local culture of using pre-school services, or do families tend to remain centred in the home?
- Will the nursery be in an attractive location?
- Is it somewhere parents will want to bring their children? For example, parents may be put off if the nursery is on a main road or adjacent to a railway line or rubbish tip.
- Is the local area child-friendly? Generally families gravitate towards areas which have good facilities for children and make it easy for families to do things.

DETERMINING SUPPLY

The purpose of this is to find out what childcare is offered in the area, whether there is sufficient to meet the demand from parents, and whether the childcare offered is what parents are looking for in terms of opening hours, fees, age groups, location and quality. Typical questions to ask include:

- What do local nurseries offer?
- What age groups are catered for?
- What opening hours are offered?
- How many places do the existing nurseries have?
- What staff:child ratios do they use?
- Are their staff qualified?
- What is their nursery philosophy?
- What are their premises like?
- Are they safe and clean?
- Are they accessible?
- What are their fees?
- Do they have a waiting list?
- What do other forms of childcare offer?
- Are there any playgroups?
- When are they open?
- What do the children do there?
- Do parents have to help on a rota basis?
- How many registered childminders are there in the area?
- Do many of the childminders have vacancies?
- Is it easy to find a childminder?
- Are they supported by the local authority with training, equipment grants etc.?
- What do the childminders charge?
- What advantages are there for parents who use a nanny? Is it easy for them to find a nanny to work in the area?
- Do any of the local schools have nursery classes?
- How many such places are available?
- Do they have extended day sessions for working parents?

- Are there any other forms of childcare with which you will have to compete?
- Are there any gaps in local childcare services which provide an opportunity for a differentiated service?
- Are there any age groups for which there are few places (usually under-twos)?
- Are all the nurseries open sufficiently long hours (e.g. 8.00 a.m. to 6.00 p.m.) to meet the needs of working parents?
- Are there any areas in the locality where there are few nurseries?
- Are all the nurseries of a similar philosophy (e.g. Montessori) and is there potential for you to differentiate on this basis?

WHERE TO OBTAIN THE INFORMATION

It is important to talk to as many people as possible who are involved in local childcare as users (parents and local employers), as providers (state, voluntary and private) and as professionals (GPs, health visitors and daycare officers) in order to build up a picture of local needs and childcare provision. There are several steps you can take.

Contact the local authority registration unit

The officers in the local authority registration and inspection unit will be in a good position to give you an overall picture of childcare provision in the area. They will know how many nurseries there are, whether there are any age groups for which there are few places, whether the nurseries have waiting lists, and roughly what level of fees they charge. Most local authorities will be able to provide you with a list of local nurseries in all sectors.

You should also ask for a copy of the local authority guidelines for registration of nurseries, so that you are informed about their specific requirements for nursery provision (such as space, staffing ratios etc.). It is useful to ask the registration and inspection unit for the most recent Children's Services Plan and the Early Years Partnership Plan, which set out the local plans and issues for childcare. There may also be reports or studies published on local childcare provision. It is also important to talk to the local authority education department.

Local authority registration officers will be limited in the time they can spend giving information, so it is best to use their available time wisely, and plan the questions you would like to ask. If there is a childcare information network in your area, you could use that service as an alternative source of information about local provision.

Obtain statistics on the local area

Local population data, labour statistics and economic plans can usually be obtained from the local authority economic development unit (or similar department). It is also worth obtaining the local authority Unitary Development Plan as this contains useful statistics and explains where the local authority is seeking to direct investment, what services they hope to develop and the principles they are applying to planning applications (which will be relevant if you are seeking to change the use of premises from office, residential or retail use). The local Chamber of Commerce or the local Training and Enterprise Council (TEC) may also have useful information, statistics or reports.

Contact local parent groups

Parent groups, such as the National Childbirth Trust, provide an easy way of contacting parents to find out what kind of childcare they are looking for and whether or not it is available. You may be able to talk to the Chair or Secretary over the telephone, or perhaps arrange to attend a group meeting and chat to parents informally. They will be able to tell you a lot about local childcare. These groups may also have regular newsletters in which you could advertise your nursery. The parents will also be able to tell you where parents look for information about nurseries, which will help you plan your advertising when you open your nursery.

Find out about ethnic minority groups in the area

From an equal opportunities perspective you should make sure you find out about ethnic minority groups in the area, and assess how you might ensure that your nursery meets their needs. This information will also help you plan for ethnic minorities in your recruitment, nursery literature, menus etc. You should also find out what advice the local authority can offer on good practice in equal opportunities.

Contact local professionals

You will find that there are many professionals involved with children and their families, e.g. GPs, practice nurses, health visitors and school teachers. They will all have a perspective on childcare, and may be able to help you find out about local provision and what is missing. Health Visitors can be a helpful source of referrals if you will be offering places for babies in your nursery.

Look at noticeboards

Local noticeboards can provide a wealth of useful information. There will be adverts for other nurseries, so you will be able to find out about them and observe how they present themselves. Parents may be advertising for childcarers, so you will be able to gauge what parents are seeking, and how easily they find it. If you see childminders advertising you may deduce that there are childminder vacancies with which you must compete.

Contact all local nurseries

It is a worthwhile investment of time to contact all the nurseries in your area, at least by telephone. This will enable you to find out what services they offer, at what fees, to establish the availability of places, and to find out how they present themselves to prospective parents – are they welcoming and do they sound as though they know what they are doing? If at all possible you should try to visit at least a few to get a feel for the overall quality of local provision and how you will position your nursery in the local childcare market place.

Key questions	Possible sources
Assessing demand	
■ Size of under-fives population	Children's Services Plan, Early Years Partnership Plan
■ Employment/unemployment rates	Unitary Development Plan, Census
■ Numbers of working parents	Unitary Development Plan, Census
■ Local usage of nurseries, etc.	Children's Services Plan, Observation from noticeboards
■ Local work patterns	Unitary Development Plan, Census
■ Local prosperity	Unitary Development Plan, Observation
■ Large employers seeking nursery places	Chamber of Commerce, Registration and Inspection Unit, TEC
■ Attractiveness of location	Observation
■ Access to local transport	Observation
■ Availability of children's facilities	Observation, Children's Services Plan
Determining supply	
■ Names of local nurseries, etc.	Registration and Inspection Unit, Education Department, Early Years Department, Childcare Information Network (if available), Notice boards
■ Services offered by local nurseries, nursery schools and LEA nursery schools and classes	Telephone contact and visits, Local parent groups
■ Services offered by playgroups	Telephone contact and visits, Local parents groups
■ Services offered by childminders	Registration and Inspection Unit, Local parent groups
■ Services offered by nannies	Nanny agencies, Local parent groups
■ Gaps in local provision	Children's Services Plan, Registration and Inspection Unit, Local professionals, Test advert

Local market research information sources

Run a test advert

It is worth considering a test advert for your proposed nursery. This is a good way to test the likely level of genuine interest in your nursery. You will need to think about:

■ what telephone number you will ask parents to contact
■ who will answer the telephone
■ what you will say to parents
■ what information you will have ready to send to them.

Adverts could be placed in a local newspaper, in the newsletter of a local parents' group, on the noticeboard at a local library or other community facility, or in children's clothes shops.

WATCH POINT

If you run a test advert you will need to word your advert carefully to be sufficiently concrete for parents to respond, and yet not misleading, e.g. not suggesting that the nursery is now open.

Contact local employers

If you have any large employers in your chosen area, you could contact them to find out whether or not they would be interested in purchasing places in your nursery. You could also talk to them about how easy or difficult it is for their employees to find local childcare. It is usually appropriate to contact the Personnel Manager in the first instance. The switchboard will be able to tell you this person's name. The person to whom you speak will probably ask you to send them information about the nursery, so you should have this prepared in advance.

Preparing a market research report

By the end of your research you should have developed a picture of your intended service offering – age groups, hours, full-time or sessional places, nursery philosophy and fees – and the typical family you are aiming to attract. This will be invaluable to you in preparing your detailed business plan and your marketing plan for your nursery.

The extent to which you decide to document your research and conclusions will depend on whether or not you will be approaching a bank or an outside investor for finance. As a minimum you should aim to prepare a statement for yourself of the following items:

■ your proposed service offering
■ the typical family you are aiming to target
■ a list of other local nurseries and what they offer
■ how you propose to compete with other local nurseries.

If you are seeking outside finance, it would be worth writing up a full report of your findings to present to a potential investor. Such a report could be attached to a business plan or an investment proposal, and the main points summarised in the main part of the business plan or investment proposal.

CASE STUDY: CHADWICK LODGE

This case study offers an example of the information which is typically included in a market research report for a nursery.

Chadwick Lodge is a large Edwardian house in a residential suburb of a metropolitan area. The owner has no children, but has noticed a nursery near his home which appears to be very busy. He has made some initial enquiries about childcare, and has concluded that there is a shortage. He therefore wishes to examine in detail the potential for a nursery at Chadwick Lodge. He has commissioned a firm of specialist consultants to carry out a detailed market research study for him. Some of the information they have prepared for him is summarised below as an example of the information you should expect to gather and analyse.

Summary of main findings

Places in private nurseries for children under two are in very short supply locally. This presents an opportunity to fill a gap in existing provision by offering places for babies, perhaps even concentrating primarily on gaining a strong reputation for caring for babies in the first year of opening Chadwick Lodge.

Although most of the local nurseries have vacancies for children over two years, those which seem to offer the better standards of care and/or are in the more affluent area to the west of Chadwick Lodge are full or close to full. There appears to be a basis for competing with existing nurseries by establishing a reputation for good quality childcare and communicating this effectively in advertising, nursery literature and personal contact with parents.

Parents appear to recognise the link between cost and standards, evidenced by the nurseries which offer a better service charging higher fees and having fewer vacancies. It is likely, therefore, to be viable to offer a premium service.

Most local private nurseries are open from 8.00 a.m. to 6.00 p.m. There is, therefore, an opportunity for service differentiation by opening slightly longer hours, say 8.00 a.m. to 6.15 p.m.

It seems likely that there are professional families living within the Chadwick Lodge catchment area who would be target users of the nursery. However, this should be confirmed by test advertising.

There is unlikely to be significant demand for nursery places from local employers, most being small businesses, and the larger employers having their own workplace nurseries. There is no evidence to indicate that local employers are reserving places in nurseries.

Other parties apparently have plans to open new nurseries or expand locally, indicating that they have a positive view of the demand for nursery places. As some of these will be close to Chadwick Lodge, it will be important to monitor their progress and to establish the basis on which Chadwick Lodge will compete.

The consultants provided detailed information to support their conclusions, covering all the issues discussed above. They also gathered useful information on expansion plans and vacancies by contacting local nurseries, which enabled them to prepare the following tables of information.

Type of nursery	Total within 2.0 miles	Within 0.5 miles	0.5–1.0 miles	1.0–1.5 miles	1.5–2.0 miles
Private	10	1	2	2	5
Private term-time only	21	1	4	6	10
Private creche	1	0	0	1	0
Voluntary	17	2	3	4	8
Total	49	4	9	13	23

Proximity of each type of nursery to Chadwick Lodge

Location	Extra child numbers		When?	Proximity (miles)
	Under 2	Over 2		
The Avenue	0	36	Sept this year	0.25
Fairway	12	24	In 12 months	1.50
CatkinLane	0	15	Jan next year	1.20
Saville Road	10	0	Sept this year	0.50
Priory Hill	9	21	Next year?	1.75

Known expansion plans of nurseries in close proximity to Chadwick Lodge

Age group	Current places	Planned places	Total forecast
Under 2 years	35	31	66
Over 2 years	270	96	366
Total	305	127	432

Total estimated private nursery places by age group

They also prepared a diagrammatic map of nurseries within a two-mile radius of Chadwick Lodge to present a picture of the pattern of nursery provision in the area, and the proximity of competition.

Example of service offering
Chadwick Lodge Nursery will provide full daycare for babies from 6 months old, toddlers and pre-school children up to the age of five years.

The nursery will be open to children 8.00 a.m. to 6.15 p.m. Monday to Friday 51 weeks per year.

Nursery	Weekly fees			Hours		Proximity	Comments
	Under 2	2–3	3–5	Open	Close	Miles	
Oak Park Nursery	n/a	£75	£75	8.00am	5.30pm	1.6	30 places. Full.
Honey Nursery	n/a	£65	£65	8.00am	5.30pm	1.0	12–15 places. Vacancies. Poor presentation
ABC Nursery	£120	£100	£80	8.00am	6.00pm	0.5	30 places. New nursery. Some vacancies for 3–5s
Hazel Dene Nursery	n/a	£90	£75	8.00am	5.30pm	1.5	40 places. Full.
Blackbird Nursery	£125	£100	£85	8.00am	6.15pm	1.75	30 places. Full
St. Michael's Nursery (Montessori)	n/a	£90	£90	8.00am	5.30pm	1.8	30 places. Full.
Child's Place Nursery	£90	£90	£90	7.30am	6.00pm	0.75	50 places. Vacancies for 2–5s
Bedford Square Nursery	n/a	£60	£60	8.30am	5.30pm	1.25	25 places. Full
Rosie's' Day Nursery	n/a	£100	£75	8.00am	5.30pm	1.6	20 places. Vacancies from September
St. Mary's Nursery	n/a	£110	£85	7.30am	6.00pm	0.25	35 places. Full

Summary of private nurseries within a two-mile radius of Chadwick Lodge

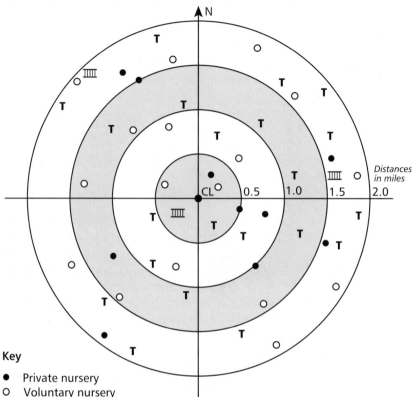

Key

- ● Private nursery
- ○ Voluntary nursery
- **T** Term-time only nursery,
  including LEA nursery schools and classes
- **CL** Chadwick Lodge
- ⛫ Rail links

Nurseries within a two-mile radius of Chadwick Lodge

Full-time and part-time places will be available. The nursery sessions will run from 8.00 a.m. to 1.00pm and from 1.30 p.m. to 6.15 p.m.

The nursery environment is to be happy, safe and stimulating for children in all age groups.

The nursery will offer a pre-school curriculum which prepares children for Key Stage 1 of the National Curriculum.

Quality in the nursery will be evidenced by:

- ■ the premises, their design, flexibility and safety
- ■ the staffing ratios and staff qualifications and experience
- ■ the childcare policies (based on best practice) and the ways in which these are implemented
- ■ the reliability of the service for parents
- ■ the employment policies, aimed at ensuring a stable and motivated nursery team to give continuity of care for the children.

Fees will be set by reference to the cost of providing care for each age group, and the fees charged by other local nurseries and other competing forms of childcare.

Sample statements of competitive advantage
The nursery will offer the following advantages over a nanny or nanny share arrangement:
- reliability – the nursery will be open regardless of staff sickness
- security – all staff will have police checks
- safety – the nursery premises will be designed specifically for the purpose
- privacy – the difficulties of the employer/employee relationship in the home will not apply
- economy – the nursery will be cheaper than a sole nanny, and comparable with a nanny share
- child development – the nursery will provide opportunities for children to socialise from an early age, and to participate in a structured early learning programme, which research indicates benefits children in later life.

The nursery will aim to provide the following competitive advantages over other nurseries:
- offer places for babies (such places are scarce), which also provides the opportunity to develop loyalty from parents over several years
- maintain high standards
- employ a core team of qualified staff
- convenient location near the main area of local employment
- easy access to the nursery premises, including off–street parking
- security within a development with electronic security gates
- good-sized outdoor play space.

Details of competing nurseries are given in the table on page 15.

Conclusion

Your market research will, hopefully, have given you the confidence to proceed with your plans for a nursery. You should now have a clear picture of the childcare service sector nationally and its potential for growth, and of the pattern of local childcare with which you will have to compete. You should also have a clear view of how you will differentiate your childcare service from others, and attract parents to your nursery, and an appreciation of the typical levels of nursery fees in your local market place. All of this information will be used as you proceed with and build on your plans.

CHECKLIST

Assessing demand
- Large under-five population?
- Low unemployment?
- Large numbers of working parents?

- Prosperity?
- Large employers who might purchase places?
- Large inbound working population?
- Local culture of using nursery care?
- Local culture of using pre-school services?
- Attractive location?
- Child-friendly area?

Determining supply
- What do local nurseries offer?
  Age groups
  Hours
  Staff ratios
  Qualifications
  Nursery philosophy
  Fees
- What do other forms of childcare offer?
  Playgroups
  Childminders
  Nannies
  Nursery classes in schools
- Are there waiting lists?
- What are the possible gaps?
  Age groups
  Hours
  Geography
  Services

Sources of information
- Census data (census office and local authority)
- Local authority Unitary Development Plan
- Local Chamber of Commerce
- Local authority reviews of childcare provision
- Local Registration and Inspection Unit
- Local professionals
- Local parent groups
- Local nanny agencies
- Personnel officers of local employers
- Noticeboards (adverts for and of childcare services)

Action points
- Collect information, collate and analyse
- Contact all local nurseries
- Contact Local Registration and Inspection Unit
- Contact local employers
- Contact local parents
- Test advertise

2 ACQUIRING PREMISES

What this chapter covers:
- **Specifying premises requirements**
- **Searching for premises**
- **Obtaining planning consent**
- **Obtaining title to your premises**

> *Apparently small details should not be ignored, for it is only through them that large designs are possible.*
>
> St Jerome

This chapter offers guidance and ideas on how to find suitable premises for your nursery. We suggest issues you should think about when specifying your premises requirements, how to find out about premises which are available, and what to do when you have found the right premises.

Finding suitable premises is one of the most difficult aspects of starting a nursery. You will have a very specific list of requirements, and you will need to find premises which either have planning consent for use as a nursery, or for which you will be able to obtain planning consent for a change of use. This can be a difficult and lengthy process.

Specifying premises requirements

It is important not to compromise over premises. Some premises are simply not suited for use as a nursery, and attempting to adapt them may lead to serious operational problems later. Further, a good location for premises is often the key to the success of any business, and this is no less true for a nursery.

Exercising caution and taking time in choosing premises for a nursery is a good idea. In addition to the issues about locations and catchment area, you should also be assured that an effective nursery can be run within the space provided by the site, and that the premises can be built or converted to meet all the requirements. Unless it is possible to ensure that all the facilities necessary for the nursery can be provided, it is not appropriate to proceed.

Houses, prefabs, unused school buildings, defunct factories and purpose built structures are all frequently used for nurseries. They offer different possibilities, reflecting alternative philosophies about community expectations and about childcare. Each structure will offer some bonuses and some limitations. These include:
- room size
- number of rooms
- arrangement of services

Different structures will offer some bonuses and some limitations

- proximity of toilets to activity areas
- stairs
- hazards
- garden and outdoor space
- storage
- natural light sources.

Before making a choice it is crucial to visualise how the building will impact on the operational plan for the nursery and whether or not the options offered are compatible with the nursery's intended objectives and quality standards.

It is sensible to draw up a list of your premises requirements. This will serve as a checklist against which to assess any suitable premises, and will also be useful to pass on to anyone who may be helping you locate premises.

Renting or purchasing

Whether you wish to rent or to purchase a property will probably be determined by your access to finance. For example, you may find that a bank will lend you sufficient money to operate in rented premises, but will be unwilling to finance the purchase of a property, at least as your first business venture.

Proximity to catchment area

You will want premises which are located in your desired catchment area (determined by reference to your market research). This may be a specific area or areas, perhaps near a particular school, office development, train station or other amenities.

Access to transport

Easy access to public transport for parents who are working is generally highly desirable. Without it parents will find it difficult to use the nursery unless they live and work within walking distance of the nursery or can drive to work.

Parking and traffic

Adequate parking spaces and an accessible dropping off point are important. If you need to apply for planning consent, these are essential, and your premises should be situated in a road where traffic flows and congestion will not be a problem.

Adequate space

You will need to check with your local authority registration unit the requirements for the size of activity areas per child enrolled. These are as follows:

- each child of 0–2 years needs 3.7 m^2 (40 sq. ft.)
- each child of 2–3 years needs 2.8 m^2 (30 sq. ft.)
- each child of 3–5 years needs 2.5 m^2 (25 sq. ft.).

Suitable or adaptable indoor space

This is where the vision of how the nursery will operate becomes significant. Too many rooms are hard to supervise and demand high staff numbers. A few very large rooms present difficulties for offering a range of provision and helping children to feel comfortable.

Ground floor level

At least one floor should be on ground floor level. Premises which are solely on the ground floor level are preferable.

Disabled access

Your nursery should have space which is accessible for people with disabilities, or can be adapted easily (entrances, parking, access, toilets, light sources, movement within the building and emergency exits).

Outdoor playspace

Outdoor playspace of an adequate size in relation to the indoor space is essential. The registration requirements frequently specify the size of the area needed (check with your local authority). Usually for each child of 0–5 years 18 m^2 (190 sq. ft.) of outdoor space are needed. However, consideration must be given to what the space can accommodate, what activities will take place in the garden, and how each group of children will use their outdoor time in each season of the year. Good practice suggests that thought and investment must be allocated to the garden and outdoor areas.

Access to parks

If the size of the outdoor space attached to the premises is very restricted, are there any suitable parks close to the nursery? The opportunities for access to parks, including use by other sectors of the community, will impact on how useful this might be to the nursery. The significance for the daily routine and staffing levels should not be overlooked.

Searching for premises

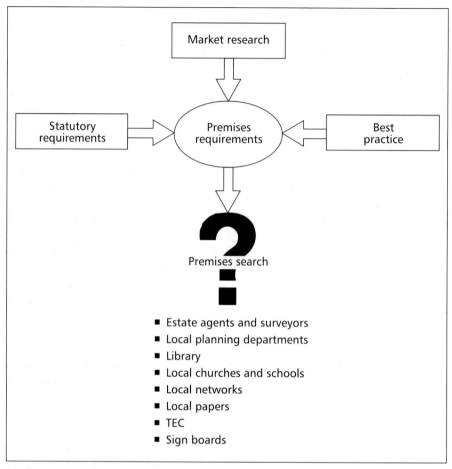

Market research

Statutory requirements → Premises requirements ← Best practice

?

Premises search

- Estate agents and surveyors
- Local planning departments
- Library
- Local churches and schools
- Local networks
- Local papers
- TEC
- Sign boards

Finding suitable premises

In searching for premises it is sensible to spread your net as widely as possible. You will find you have to work very hard at this. Each area is different, but typically you could consider any or all of the following.

Local estate agents and surveyors
Contact local estate agents and surveyors. Give them your list of requirements, and keep in close contact with them. They should have detailed knowledge of the local market, and may be able to make suggestions about properties even if they are not acting for the vendor or landlord.

Local planning department
Contact the local planning department. They may know of properties which have planning consent for use as a nursery, and will be able to explain the local

authority's policy on change of use, e.g. in some areas there is a shortage of housing stock so that the local authority is reluctant to sanction change of use from residential to non-residential. They will also be able to give you a view on the roads for which a nursery is unlikely to cause a traffic flow problem (and hence there is a greater chance of receiving planning consent).

Library
Consult the local authority Unitary Development Plan. This should be available in the local library, and will provide information about the local authority planning policies.

Local churches and schools
Contact local churches and schools. Premises which have existing use for educational purposes, and church halls, fall into the same planning category as nurseries. It is therefore easier to obtain planning consent for these premises as a nursery. However, you should think very carefully about taking on any premises where you will have shared use, e.g. a church hall which is used by other organisations in the evenings, as this will have implications for the type of nursery service you offer. For example, it is almost impossible to offer full daycare for babies and toddlers in shared premises because of the facilities you will need (laundry, nappy change area and kitchen) and because of the difficulties in maintaining hygiene standards when the facilities are shared.

Local network
Use any local networks to which you may have access. These could be personal friends, local business people, or voluntary sector networks – anyone who may know about the availability of premises.

Local papers
Read the local papers. There may be adverts for premises, or you may pick up useful information, e.g. a new office development in which you may be able to rent space for a nursery.

Local TEC
Contact your local Training and Enterprise Council (TEC). TECs aim to support the development of new businesses in the area, and may have information about premises which are available.

Sign boards
Look out for sign boards indicating that premises are vacant. It is worth investing time walking the area to gain a better understanding of the specific streets in which you are interested, and to spot possible opportunities for premises.

WATCH POINT

Once the nursery premises have been chosen in principle, it may be helpful and cost effective to have a feasibility study carried out by an independent consultant, who can investigate the registration and operational planning issues as well as offer indicative budget figures.

Obtaining planning consent

Planning approval is required to allow the premises to be used as a nursery. The local authority planning department will focus on issues such as changes to the external appearance of the premises, potential nuisance factors, road traffic, parking facilities, noise and proximity of other community facilities within the authority's Unitary Development Plan.

If it is proposed to use part of the nursery premises for domestic accommodation, then there will be additional factors for each of the regulatory authorities to consider.

You would be well advised to obtain planning consent before committing to the purchase or lease of any premises. The planning consent must be specifically for a day nursery for children under five years. In order to apply for planning consent you will need to complete an application form available from your local authority planning department, and they will require architect's drawings. Before investing any money commissioning an architect to complete these drawings, you need to be reasonably sure that planning consent will be granted.

It is therefore worth holding preliminary discussions with the planning officer, the Registration and Inspection Unit and the fire and environmental health departments. You should also consider potential objections from local residents, such as the effect on parking, traffic and noise. Your architect will be able to help you with this, and should also be experienced in negotiating with planning officers to give your application the best chance of success – if the planning officer does not support the application it is unlikely that the council members will approve it.

WATCH POINT

- It can take a long time to obtain planning consent. Allow for this in your plans.
- Establish the likelihood of obtaining planning consent before commissioning architect's drawings.

Planning consent can take several months to come through, so be prepared for a wait. If your application is successful, the consent should be in writing and should be retained. If it is unsuccessful you should discuss this with the planning officer before considering an appeal. Again, your architect should be able to help you assess whether or not it is worth appealing.

Some planning consents are given subject to specific conditions, e.g. for a limited number of years, to a specific person, or restrictions on the use of outdoor space at certain times of day. Any of these may have implications for the way in which you operate your nursery, or for opportunities to sell your nursery at a later date, and you should therefore be quite certain that you are aware of and comfortable with these restrictions.

Obtaining title to your premises

Once you have found your premises and obtained planning consent, you will need to complete the legal formalities. The process is slightly different according to whether you are purchasing a freehold or a leasehold property, but for either type of transaction you should engage a solicitor to advise you and deal with the conveyancing.

Freehold
If you are purchasing a freehold property you will need to consider the same issues as you would if you were purchasing a residential house, and would be advised to commission a detailed survey and valuation. The purchase process should be broadly the same as a normal house purchase, and your solicitor will be able to guide you through the process.

Leasehold
A leasehold will probably be a commercial lease for a specified number of years. You will need to agree the basic terms up-front, such as the length of the lease, the annual rent, any rent-free period or any premium payable. It may be sensible to ask a firm of chartered surveyors to help you with these negotiations, and to advise you on other issues such as the terms of future rent reviews. When you are happy with the basic terms, you should go through the lease with your solicitor. It may contain certain clauses with which you as a tenant will have to comply. You will need to make sure that these are compatible with a nursery. They may include an obligation to restrict noise levels, restrictions on the use of outdoor space, restrictions on the times at which you can use the premises (e.g. not at weekends), or restrictions on access to the nursery to one specific entrance.

You should also be aware that, under English law, if you assign the lease you remain liable for any rent unpaid by the person to whom you sell the lease; you are therefore taking on a long-term commitment which may extend beyond the period for which you run the nursery. (This may be changed in the near future by legislation; check the position with your solicitor.)

With a leasehold you should make sure that you are happy with the arrangements for paying rent and service charges, and build these into your business plan. You should also make sure that you understand the basis of future rent reviews and are happy with this.

WATCH POINTS

- You should not take on any premises without consulting a solicitor first.
- Make sure you have planning consent to use your premises as a nursery before you sign a lease or purchase a freehold.

Rates
You will be liable to pay the uniform business rates on your premises. These can be quite substantial, and you should budget for them in your business plan.

When you open the nursery, the Inland Revenue valuers will assess the premises and determine the rateable value. The rates are then calculated on the pence in the pound rate for the relevant fiscal year.

You can appeal against the assessment if you think it is too high, and must do so within a certain time of receiving the valuation (details of the current position are available from your local Inland Revenue valuation office). Some firms of chartered surveyors specialise in acting for clients on rate valuation appeals, and will usually charge fees on a success basis.

You can also apply for discretionary relief up to 20 per cent, or for hardship relief if you are making a loss. Applications should be made to your local authority rating department, and they will tell you what information to provide.

Insurance

You should take out an insurance policy to insure your premises from the time you exchange contracts. You will also need to have public and employer's liability insurance in place before you open your nursery. Policies are available specially for nurseries, and include insurance for premises, contents, public liability and employer's liability and other optional cover.

Conclusion

Searching for premises may take some time and prove very frustrating, but if you start with a clear list of your requirements, apply ingenuity and use all your contacts to the full, you should find the right premises in the right area which will work well for you as the home for your new venture.

CHECKLIST

Searching for premises
- Outline specification
- Local estate agents and surveyors
- Local planning department
- Local authority Unitary Development Plan
- Local churches and schools
- Local networks
- Local papers
- Training and Enterprise Council
- Sign boards

Obtaining planning consent
- Views of Planning Officer
- Views of Registration Officer
- Views of Fire Officer
- Views of Environmental Health Officer
- Traffic and other local considerations

CHECKLIST continued

- Architect's drawings
- Applications

Purchasing freehold
- Engage solicitor
- Agree terms
- Full survey
- Planning consent
- Draft contract
- Normal enquiries
- Other as directed by solicitor
- Insurance

Entering into a leasehold agreement
- Engage solicitor
- Term, length of lease etc.
- Planning consent
- Restriction clauses
- Rent reviews
- Service charges
- Other clauses as advised by solicitor
- Insurance

Paying rates
- Inland Revenue valuation
- Rates bill from local authority
- Valuation appeal
- Discretionary or hardship relief application

3 *BUSINESS PLANNING*

What this chapter covers:
■ Elements of a business plan
■ The operational plan
■ The marketing plan
■ Track record
■ The implementation plan
■ The financial plan
■ Risk analysis

Fail to plan and plan to fail.

Old English saying

This chapter is about planning – not just thinking about your plans, but articulating and documenting them in detail. We examine the components of a good business plan, and explain how to approach the sometimes daunting task of pulling your plans together, and we concentrate on some of the detail of putting together a business plan specifically for a nursery. This chapter looks at your business plan as a document which you will use to guide you through the early days of your nursery, and which will also be vital in securing financial and other support for your nursery.

Elements of a business plan

Your business plan should be your route map through the start-up phase of your nursery, and throughout the on-going management of your business. The plan should bring together all the things you are going to do, noting the most important ones on which the success of your nursery will depend, and should serve as a reminder to you of these. It will be well worth looking back at your business plan some months into your new venture, monitoring your progress and, if necessary, revisiting and revising your plan – things generally never turn out quite as planned.

Within your overall business plan, you should include a detailed financial plan. Money will almost inevitably be one of your key resources and you will have to manage it well and spend it wisely. Your financial plan will help you do this provided you monitor progress against your plan and, where there are discrepancies, find out why these have occurred.

A business plan will also serve as an essential document to convince a potential investor or lender of the viability of your proposed nursery. The business

Your business plan should be your route map through the start-up phase of your nursery

plan should set out what you are going to do and how you are going to do this, including what financial and other resources you will need. A potential investor will also wish to understand why you should expect to succeed, and what risks are involved. Even if you do not require outside finance, you will need to convince yourself of all of these points.

The local authority officer dealing with your registration may ask questions about your finance and business plans. He or she needs to know that the nursery will be opened on a firm foundation, in order to protect children and families from 'belt tightening' which might affect quality standards, or from unexpected closure.

Outlines for business plans are available from most of the high street banks and local enterprise or small business agencies. These include good explanatory notes on how to put together a business plan, and are well worth studying.

Typically for a nursery there are six key elements in a business plan.

OPERATIONAL PLAN

This is the nursery 'blue-print' detailing how your nursery will operate, and forms the basis of the start-up and annual running costs in your financial plan. Details should include the age groups, opening hours, staffing, food preparation and cleaning arrangements, health and safety needs, equipment and administration. This plan should also describe the premises, and include a realistic monthly enrolment scheme with the related staff profile and salaries.

MARKETING PLAN

This should include the results of your market research, and a statement of how you intend to differentiate your service. You should explain how you intend to market your nursery, with costings. The plan should also set out your pricing policy and how this compares with your competitors.

IMPLEMENTATION PLAN

This should list each task you will need to complete before opening your nursery, and during the first six months, showing the timetable and interdependency between tasks. This will help you manage the start-up phase, when it can be quite tricky co-ordinating building work, staff recruitment, equipment purchases and delivery, marketing and advance enrolments.

TRACK RECORD

You should present your credentials and track record in both childcare and business management. Where there are any gaps in your skills you should explain how you will fill these gaps, e.g. by involving your accountant more closely in the financial management of your business if you lack business skills.

FINANCIAL PLAN

Your financial plan should include a monthly profit and loss account and monthly cash flow forecast for the start-up phase and the first two years of operation.

RISK ANALYSIS

Your plan should include a realistic assessment of what could go wrong and how you would deal with each situation or what preventative measures you could take.

HOW THE ELEMENTS FIT TOGETHER

The business plan is largely a translation exercise turning an operational model into a financial plan. Conceptually the six components fit together as follows:

Operational plan
+
Marketing plan
+
Track record
+
Implementation plan

} = {

Financial plan
+
Risk analysis

The operational plan

This really is the 'blue-print' for managing your nursery, and involves writing down how you are going to run your service. It is important to do this in order to translate what is actually going to happen in your nursery into a financial model which you will use for managing your finances. If this translation is incorrect or if the operational model is inaccurate, then you will run the risk of using up your available funds faster than you expect. That said, nothing ever goes exactly according to plan, so you should expect to build some contingencies into your financial model.

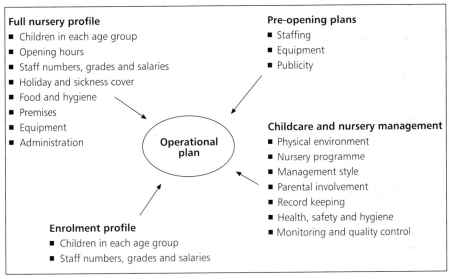

Input to an operational plan

The two most critical factors which will influence your financial plan are the enrolments and the staffing. For this reason many nurseries concentrate on monitoring the 'gross margin' (nursery fees less staff costs) when keeping track of their financial performance.

THE FULL NURSERY

First you will need details about the nursery when it is eventually full. These will be used as the basis for your long-term cost structure and the calculation of your fees on a cost plus basis (see also suggestions on setting fees below). The details you will need are as follows:

- the age groups of the children in the nursery when it is full – based on your actual or expected registration details
- the opening hours, which will influence other factors such as the staff shift

patterns and staff numbers. They will also affect the market sectors you can serve, and this needs to be explained in your business plan

- the number of staff in each role and grade who you will need to employ when the nursery is full, together with expected salary ranges
- the number of weeks of staff cover you expect to have to provide for staff holidays and sickness, and the weekly cost of staff cover (e.g. local agency rates). You will know how much holiday entitlement you are offering, but you will need to make some assumptions about staff sickness
- food preparation and cleaning arrangements. These will affect your staffing levels or contract costs as well as the cost of raw materials, such as food and cleaning materials
- premises and expected running costs. Do you have to pay a service charge? Are the premises likely to need a lot of maintenance?
- equipment needs – you will need an annual budget for replacing old equipment and adding to your stock. You should also think about the activity programme you are planning to run and how this will affect your budget. For example, if you are planning to include a French activity using an outside specialist, you will need to budget for this
- administration needs. What records will you keep? What will you need in order to do this? For example, child profile books will cost money to produce, and you need to make sure you have a budget for them.

ENROLMENT PROFILE

You will also need to think about how your nursery will develop from initially having no children or staff to a full nursery. Typically you will need the following

It is not good practice to enrol large groups of children together

information in order to translate the expected operation into a financial plan for the first two years:

- the enrolment profile as the nursery places fill, remembering that it is not good practice to enrol large groups of children together. You should be very realistic and over-conservative about this, as it takes time to establish a nursery's reputation. You may also find that you fill places in one age group quickly, especially if you are offering baby places, but then take some time to attract children from the other age groups
- the expected number of staff and their roles and grades, with expected salaries, to match the enrolment plan. When you open you will need a core team of four or five staff in order to cover the shift patterns and to provide sufficient cover in the event of an emergency, no matter how few children are enrolled
- the local authority registration requirements for the child numbers, staff qualifications, in-service training, and any matters which will affect your costs. The basic requirements are in The Children Act, Guidance, Volume 2, and these are supplemented by the local authority guidelines
- the period of time prior to opening when you plan to employ your staff. They will need time to familiarise themselves with the nursery lay-out, and to plan together how they will work as a team and with you
- what publicity you are planning prior to opening and in the first year. You will need a good budget for this in order to ensure that you spread the word about your nursery as widely as possible. You will also need to have plenty of information printed about your nursery ready to send out to interested parents
- the equipment you plan to purchase prior to opening and then into the first year. You may decide to phase your purchases so that you can buy according to the needs and interests of the children who actually enrol.

GOOD PRACTICE

In your operational plan you should also document briefly how you intend to manage your nursery and establish good practice. This is to provide investors or lenders with an outline of how you will operate, and the factors which will be important to your success. This will also provide you with a reference point and reminder of what you are aiming to achieve. There are a number of ways of organising this information, but usually the following sub-headings work well:

- Physical environment and ambience
- Nursery programme – care and curriculum
- Staff – recruitment, selection, pay and conditions
- Management style
- Parental involvement
- Equipment
- Catering, nutrition and food handling
- Hygiene, health and safety

- Record keeping and information
- Monitoring and quality control.

All of these matters are examined in detail in other chapters, and you will need to prepare detailed policies and procedures for each of them. With reference to the operational plan, it is important to identify any financial implications of the way you decide to or are required to operate, in order to prepare a realistic financial plan.

The marketing plan

Marketing, and how to put together a marketing plan are dealt with in Chapter 1. However, your business plan should summarise the results and conclusions from your market research, and detail how you plan to market your business. You should also make sure you identify how much you will need to spend on marketing material and advertising both initially and on-going. You should also think about your marketing in detail, and how you plan to go about it, to make sure that you have everything ready when you need it.

Track record

Make sure you can demonstrate the right skills

An investor or lender will want to know that you have the right skills and experience in order to set up and manage a nursery. These will include both childcare and business skills. It is worth spending some time assessing your own skills, or your combined skills if you are part of a team, to make sure that you have all the angles covered. If there is any area in which you do not feel confident, think about how you can address this. By doing this you will avoid possible mistakes at a later date, as well as being able to present yourself and/or your team confidently to possible investors.

The implementation plan

Starting a nursery involves a complex interplay of a lot of tasks. Planning these is vital, even at a high level. It is worth trying to list every task you can imagine you will have to complete, and looking at their dependencies (which ones you have to complete before you can start another one) and timings. By doing this you should be able to avoid mistakes, and ensure that everything comes together at the right time. For example, you will want to open your nursery as soon as possible after the premises are finished, but this means making sure that you have recruited staff in time, and that you have at least some children enrolled in the nursery. This alone requires careful co-ordination of recruitment and staff matters, building work and marketing.

You may find it helpful to group your tasks under certain headings. Typically the following work well:

- Staff selection and recruitment
- Staff induction
- Building and equipment
- Registration
- Operations
- Finance
- Marketing
- Opening.

An example of an implementation plan is set out on pages 36–37. The circumstances of each nursery are different, and your plan will need to be individualised. However, there are some general pointers which you may find useful to consider in planning the start-up of your nursery.

STAFF SELECTION AND RECRUITMENT

Staff selection and recruitment needs about 15 weeks as a minimum. This is to allow sufficient time to place adverts, short-list candidates, arrange and hold first and second interviews, make offers, and give staff sufficient time to serve their notice in their existing employment.

BUILDING WORK

It is worth tying builders to penalty clauses so that they have an incentive to finish their work on time. However, in practice builders seldom finish to the timetable, and usually leave a mess to clear up. It is worth taking this into account in your plans.

SEASONAL VARIATION IN ENROLMENT

Nursery operators have found that there are good and bad times of the year to open a nursery. There appear to be certain months in which parents think about

—— Weeks before opening ——   —— Weeks after opening ——

	16	15	14	13	12	11	10	9	8	7	6	5	4	3	2	1	0	1	2	3	4	5	6	7	8	9	10	11

Staff selection and recruitment
Finalise job specifications
Finalise person specifications
Finalise all papers for shortlisted candidates
Finalise recruitment programme
Design adverts
Place adverts
Short-list and arrange interviews
Hold interviews for Manager and Deputy
Second interviews
Offer letter to Manager and Deputy
Manager invited to participate in staff interviews
Hold interviews for other staff
Second interviews
Offer letter to other staff

Staff induction
Plan induction
Prepare training material
Manager in post
Deputy in post
Core team of staff in post
Induction for Manager and Deputy
Social evening for all staff
Staff induction

Building and equipment
Building work to be completed
Finalise equipment list
Establish delivery times for equipment
Negotiate terms with suppliers
Order equipment
Take delivery of equipment
Prepare nursery for opening

Example of an implementation plan

Weeks before opening | **Weeks after opening**

	16	15	14	13	12	11	10	9	8	7	6	5	4	3	2	1	0	1	2	3	4	5	6	7	8	9	10	11

Registration
(Initial discussions with Registration Unit as early as possible:
– timetable
– operating plans
– outline childcare policies)
Agree staffing with Social Services
Complete registration forms/provide information
Introduce Manager at first opportunity
Meet providers of statutory services
Provide initial list of names for police checks
Registration visit
Provide final list of names for police checks

Operations
Prepare policies and procedures
Familiarise Manager with polices and procedures
Manager and staff develop and refine procedures
Team building

Marketing
(Prepare marketing material as early as possible)
(Advertise as early as possible)
Finalise waiting list policy
Answer calls from prospective parents
Hold open evenings for prospective parents

Opening
Enrol children – administration
First group of children settle
Next group of children settle
Additional members of staff start work

Example of an implementation plan (continued)

enrolling their child in a nursery. Good opening dates are January, March, May or September. Months to avoid if you can are August, November or December. Of course it will depend when your premises become available and are finished, but you could save yourself some staff costs by delaying a November opening until January.

REGISTRATION PROCESS

You will need to find out about the registration process and its timetable in your area. These processes vary considerably in terms of the information they request and when, and the time taken to register a nursery from start to finish, but it can take up to six months. The registration officer needs to be satisfied that the children's interests and safety are protected, and that a nursery's business and professional basis is sufficiently robust to sustain an acceptable level of service over a period of years. Remember that you cannot operate without being registered.

FINANCES

It is important that you get your finances in place early on. It would be unwise to commit to responsibility for premises or to recruiting staff until you know that you will have sufficient funding either personally or from third parties in order to see your nursery through to a stable financial position.

EQUAL OPPORTUNITIES

You may find that your local TEC or registration officer can advise you about the availability of any funds which will help you fulfil your equal opportunities objectives, e.g. training resources, non-English translation and printing of material, advertising etc.

MARKETING

Allow a sensible lead in time for marketing. It can take some time to disseminate information about a new nursery, and you will need to allow for this in your schedule.

ENROLMENTS

Think about how and when you will begin to enrol children. Parents are normally happy to join a waiting list for a nursery they have never seen, but are usually reluctant to commit to a nursery until they have seen the premises and at least met the manager. How will you deal with this, given that you would like as many children as possible enrolled when you open? And just to complicate matters, parents generally want a place at a specific time (e.g. when they return to work) so will not necessarily be willing to wait until you open. You need to be quite sure that you will be able to open on the date to which you commit, or you will run the risk of creating some serious ill will among local parents.

The financial plan

It is quite a complicated business preparing a financial plan for a nursery, so it is worth spending some time up-front thinking about how you are going to set about it.

ELEMENTS OF A FINANCIAL PLAN

We have found the following an essential part of a financial plan for a nursery:
- the variables – the number of children in each age group, the staff numbers and salaries, and the enrolment pattern are the main variables which will affect your financial plan
- a costing for a full nursery – with costs allocated by age group – from which you determine your pricing (the nursery fees you propose to charge parents)
- a monthly profit and loss account, showing how much money you expect to make or lose each month for the first two years of operating
- a monthly cash flow forecast, showing your cash receipts and cash payments each month for the first two years of operating – this will also tell you how much money you will need to find from other sources
- a payback calculation to demonstrate that your nursery will be able to repay the capital invested in it, and when you expect it to do this – in other words, a check that your nursery will be a viable proposition.

PREPARING A FINANCIAL PLAN

You will need to think about how you will set about preparing a financial plan. One option may be to pay your accountant to do this, if you really feel you cannot do it yourself. However, a financial plan needs to be a 'living plan', updated as your nursery gets underway, and you will need to monitor progress against the plan on a regular basis. Apart from the cost of asking your accountant to do this, it is much better for you to get to grips with the finances of your nursery, and the financial dynamics of your business. This will enable you to have much

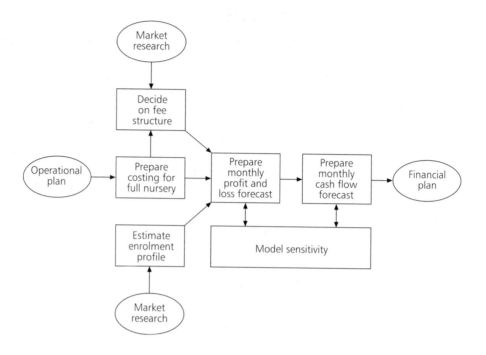

Preparing a financial plan

tighter control over your finances, which will be crucial in the first year of starting up.

There is also the danger that, as your accountant is once removed from the detailed thinking behind your plans, some crucial operational detail will be missed which may invalidate your financial plan. Another option would be to ask your accountant to get you started, but to show you how the model works so that you can take over responsibility for it.

You are strongly advised to prepare your financial plan on a computer spreadsheet programme, e.g. Lotus 1–2–3 or Excel. This will enable you to play around with the model as your plans evolve, without having to recalculate a month-by-month spreadsheet each time. Again, if you do not have the computer skills to prepare a spreadsheet, you will need to look for ways of dealing with this, e.g. your local TEC may offer a course on computer spreadsheet skills or specifically on developing financial models using a personal computer.

WATCH POINTS

When preparing a financial plan:
- ■ consider enlisting the help of an accountant
- ■ use a computer spreadsheet – do not try to do the exercise manually.

COSTING FOR A FULL NURSERY

First you should model the costs of running your nursery when it is full. This is in order to check that you will eventually be able to make a profit by charging fees to parents which more than cover the costs. You will need to decide on your own account headings, but typically those detailed below will work well for a nursery.

Most of the costs will be derived from your operational model – such as staff costs, staff cover, food, hygiene, activities – but for some you will need to make an educated guess, or try to ascertain what the costs are likely to be. For example, if you purchased your premises through an estate agent, they may be able to give an indication of the likely level of business rates. For heat and light, you could

---

Staff costs
Salaries
National Insurance
Temporary staff
Recruitment
Training

Establishment costs
Rent
Rates
Service charges
Heat and light
Maintenance and garden
Insurance

Nursery expenses
Food and drink
Activities, outings and consumables
Cleaning and hygiene
Equipment replacement
Telephone
Publicity
Administration
Staff travel
Sundry expenses

Legal, professional and finance
Legal fees
Accountancy fees
Audit fees
Interest payable
Bank charges

Central expenses
Administration
Publications and seminars
Advertising

Example of cost headings for a nursery

look at your domestic bills, and the amount of space relative to your nursery, and the expected level of usage of appliances.

You may decide to add in a cost line for depreciation. This is not an actual cash cost each year, but represents a charge each year to recover the cost of items you have paid for up-front, e.g. building work on the premises or major equipment items. You will receive value from this expenditure for some years, so it is normal practice to recover these costs over the expected life of these assets.

It is worth allocating your projected costs to each age group in order to gain a full understanding of your cost structure. This will give you a feel for the cost of providing a place for a child in each age group, and will form the basis of charging fees according to the age of a child. Many nurseries do this because of the proportionately higher cost of providing a place for a baby (with the higher staffing ratio), and to avoid baby places being subsidised by parents with older children.

PRICING

You are now in a position to think about the fees you should charge parents for using your nursery. You really need to approach this from two angles.

■ How much do you need to charge in order to cover your costs, including depreciation, and earn an acceptable profit margin? This is known as the 'cost plus' basis.

■ How much will parents pay for the service you are offering? This is known as the 'value proposition' basis. You will need to use the results of your market research to look at nurseries and other competing childcare in your area, and how much parents pay for these services.

There is no right answer – you will have to make a judgement about your fees. But it is a crucial decision. Pitch your fees too high and you may find it difficult to attract parents to your nursery. Set them too low and you will not make any money (and hence not stay in business in the long run).

	Age group		
	0–2	2–3	3–5
Cost per place per week before profit margin (£)	150.00	125.00	90.00
Required profit margin, say 10% (£)	15.00	12.50	9.00
Fees on a 'cost plus' basis (£)	165.00	137.50	99.00

Example of a pricing calculation

Nurseries usually charge a premium for part-time places because splitting a place between two or more children places an extra burden on the nursery operationally, and it is very difficult to allocate part-time places so that they use the full-time equivalent places efficiently.

The above pricing model assumes that you will eventually be able to operate at 100 per cent capacity – in other words with every place full. In practice this may be unlikely. You may wish to consider building a lower capacity into your fee structure – by calculating the cost per place on the basis of filling say 95 per cent of the places not 100 per cent.

THE MONTHLY PROFIT AND LOSS FORECAST

This will be the main model of profitability for your nursery for the first two years of operating, and is something which your financiers will look at in detail. In order to construct the model you will need the month-by-month enrolment and staffing models used in preparing your financial plan.

You can decide whether to present your profit and loss model on a cash basis or an accruals basis. A cash basis details the expenditure in each month as it is paid, whereas an accruals basis itemises expenditure as it is incurred and relates to each period. For example, you may pay rent quarterly, so on a cash basis you would itemise the rent every three months. However, this would not give a true picture of profitability because the rent is actually incurred evenly each month. Generally an accruals basis gives a more realistic picture and is to be preferred, but you may find that for some items such as the telephone, heat and light and equipment purchases, it is simpler to detail these on an 'as incurred' basis.

Once you have prepared your detailed profit and loss account, you should model its sensitivity to changes. The main variable which will affect your profitability will be enrolments. What happens to profitability if these do not grow as you expect? How low can they go before you begin to hit problems?

THE MONTHLY CASH FLOW FORECAST

This is a vital schedule, which you will find yourself going over in great detail and updating during your first year of operating and beyond. It will tell you how much cash you will have available or will need to borrow each month, and it is essential that you monitor this. Many profitable businesses have ceased to exist because they failed to monitor their cash flow. Fortunately parents are generally happy to pay fees a month in advance, so that non-payment or slow payment is not generally a problem for nurseries, but you may find that, if enrolments are slower than you expect, you have to be very careful about your cash position.

In order to prepare your cash flow forecast, you should use your profit and loss forecast, but adjust it to take account of when bills will actually be paid, not when expenditure is incurred. For example, you may pay your creditors on 30 days credit, so that some purchases will move into the following month on your cash flow forecast.

Risk analysis

Your business plan should include a realistic assessment of what could go wrong and how you would deal with each situation, or what preventative measures you could take. You should think about this carefully before embarking on your nursery project, but here are some ideas of the types of risk you should consider.

What would you do if:

- the child enrolment rate is lower than you planned?
- you quickly establish a waiting list for baby places, but have vacancies in older age groups?
- a competitor nursery opens near you?
- increased funding is provided for state nursery provision?
- one of your members of staff goes on long-term sickness?
- you find a major unexpected problem with your premises?

Conclusion

Your business plan should now be complete. It will undoubtedly have been hard work preparing it, but the time invested will pay dividends later. You should have acquired a detailed understanding of the financial dynamics of your proposed nursery, and how the operational matters impact on the finances, and vice versa. Your implementation plan will provide a step-by-step reminder of what you have to do and when, and how everything has to fit together. You should have a clear idea of your strengths and weaknesses, and how you will present yourself to any potential investors or lenders, and you should be aware of the possible risks to achieving your business plan.

CHECKLIST

Operational plan

- Ages
- Opening hours
- Staffing
- Childcare philosophy
- Premises
- Location and transport
- Equipment
- Health and safety
- Administration
- Enrolment plan and related staffing

Marketing plan

- Demand
- Supply
- Competition
- Service differentiation
- Pricing policy
- Marketing methods
- Marketing timetable
- Marketing material
- Costs

CHECKLIST continued

Implementation plan
- Staff selection and recruitment
- Staff induction
- Building and equipment
- Registration
- Operations
- Finance
- Marketing
- Opening

Track record
- Childcare experience
- Business experience
- Other sources of expertise

Financial plan
- Variables
- Full nursery costing
- Costing by age groups
- Pricing
- Monthly profit and loss forecast
- Monthly cash flow forecast

Risk analysis
- Possible risks
- Risk reduction strategies

4 FINANCE

What this chapter covers:
- **Determining finance needs**
- **Sources of finance**
- **Seeking finance**

> *Very few businesses, whether small or large, can fund all their growth from profits.*
>
> City and Inner London Training and Enterprise Council
> (now Focus Central London)

In this chapter we suggest how you might set about planning and arranging the finance for your nursery. We explore how to determine how much money you will need and what you will need it for. We look at the different types of finance which are available, and suggest how to decide which is the most suitable for your circumstances. There is no automatic access to finance – a case has to be made whatever the source. This chapter explains what to do to obtain finance for your nursery from your preferred source.

Determining finance needs

All businesses need to be underpinned with suitable finance. A nursery is no exception. Without finance which is appropriate to the business' circumstances, and which provides adequately for expansion and for the unexpected, the nursery will lack stability, with consequences for the parents and children using the service as well as for you as the owner of the business. The financial needs of your nursery should therefore be taken seriously and planned just as carefully as the childcare service offering.

FINDING THE RIGHT FINANCE PACKAGE

When planning your financial needs, the main question in your mind will probably be 'How much money will I need to get started?' However, in order to determine your particular needs, you should also think about several other questions.

Duration of financing required
You will need to think about the length of time for which you will need to borrow the money. Generally you should aim to finance long-term assets with long-term financing in order to support the financial stability of the nursery. Overdrafts, by contrast, are repayable on demand and hence are not a good form of finance for long-term assets such as premises or equipment.

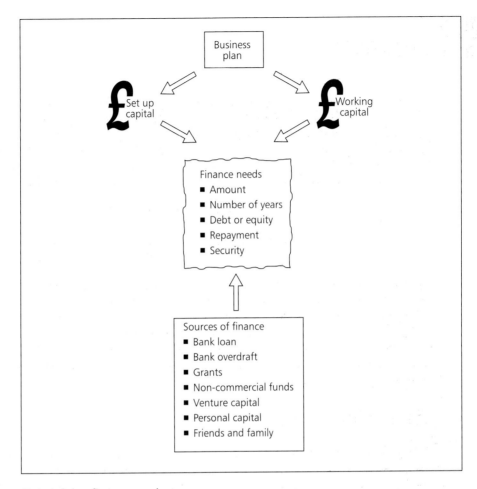

Determining finance needs

Debt or equity

You have a choice of borrowing money on which you pay interest (known as debt) and which must be repaid whether or not the nursery makes a profit, or you could raise money which gives the investor a share in the profits of the nursery (known as equity).

Security

You should think about whether you are able and willing to offer any security for the financing. This security would be used to repay the money if the nursery could not. This will almost certainly be requested by any bank from which you borrow money to finance your nursery.

Tailoring a finance package

Fixed or variable interest rate

If you are intending to raise your finance as debt, you will pay interest on your debt. This can be at a fixed rate or a variable rate of interest. Fixed interest remains the same throughout the term of the loan. Variable rates change, usually as the bank base rate goes up or down. Fixed rate loans can be useful if you wish to avoid fluctuations in your interest rate charge or if you believe that interest rates are likely to rise, but they also mean you will continue to pay the same rate even if interest rates fall.

Grant funding

Your nursery may be eligible for grant funding. It is worth taking some time to investigate this through your local TEC, your local Business Link office or the economic development department of your local authority. Grant funding has the major advantage of not being repayable, but sometimes comes with conditions attached. Alternatively preferential loans through various enterprise schemes might be worth exploring.

Personal capital

You may have any money of your own which you could use to finance all or some of the requirements. If you can avoid borrowing money from other sources it is generally better to do so, provided you have sufficient to meet the nursery's financial needs comfortably, even if the business does not develop as planned. This avoids the pressures of debt repayments and allows you to retain full control of your business. In any event most investors or banks will expect you to put at least some of your own money into your business venture.

SET-UP CAPITAL VERSUS WORKING CAPITAL

In thinking about how much money you will need when you start your nursery, it is important to distinguish between two main types of finance you will need. These are:

- set-up capital
- working capital.

Set-up capital

This is money you will need to establish your nursery, which you should recoup over time as your nursery turns to profit. It is likely, therefore, that you will need to borrow this money for some considerable time. Your business plan should contain the details you will need in order to calculate the set-up capital required, but typically the items you will need to finance from your start-up capital might include:

- initial market research
- purchase of premises or lease premium
- legal fees
- accountant's fees
- architect's fees
- consultant's fees
- premises conversion, fitting out and decoration
- equipment
- arrangement fees for finance
- marketing material and initial advertising
- staff recruitment costs (adverts, photocopying, postage)
- local authority registration fee
- charges for start up advice from the local authority
- deposits on services such as telephone, gas, electricity
- connection of telephone line
- computer and printer.

WATCH POINT

Be careful not to overlook any set-up costs. It is a good idea to allow a contingency for the unexpected.

Working capital

It is unlikely that your nursery will make a profit in its first year. Very few businesses do, and it can take quite some time for a nursery to make a profit because of the high cost structure which has to be carried on opening, regardless of the number of children attending.

As part of your business plan you will have prepared a cash flow forecast, which will tell you how much money you will need to manage your cash flows in the first two years. This is known as working capital.

In preparing your business plan you should also look at your forecasts and their sensitivities to change, in order to determine the maximum amount of money you expect to need to cover this initial period. Even after the nursery is making a profit, you may find that you still need some working capital to enable you to manage the cash flows of the business.

It is important to look at this carefully, and to look at ways of reducing your working capital. For example, you could think about:

- when you will ask parents to pay fees (normally the beginning of the month)
- when you will pay staff (normally towards the end of the month)
- when you will need to pay your PAYE/NIC to the Inland Revenue (19th of the following month)
- when you will pay your creditors (normally 30 days)
- whether or not you will ask parents to pay a deposit for their child's place and how this will affect your cash flow financing
- when your bank charges and interest payments will appear (normally quarterly)
- whether there are any expenses which could be paid monthly rather than annually, e.g. insurance or business rates.

Sources of finance

Generally there are four sources of finance you could consider:
- banks
- venture capital
- non-commercial funds
- grants.

BANKS

In the UK the high street clearing banks are probably the most useful source of finance for small businesses, generally through loans and overdrafts. They are in the business of lending money, and come under a certain amount of political pressure to support the small business sector and to help new businesses develop. In any event you will need to establish a relationship with a bank in order to open an account through which to route your money transactions. They therefore make an obvious starting point in searching for finance.

The banks generally offer two main forms of finance – term loans and overdrafts.

Term loans

Term loans, at either a fixed (pre-agreed) or a variable (changes when interest rates change) rate of interest are made for a specific number of years, usually between three and seven years, and you will be asked to pay the interest each month and to make a repayment of capital each month.

The loans are usually structured so that you pay more interest in the first few years, and repay more capital in the final years, but the monthly repayment remains constant.

It is sometimes possible to negotiate a 'repayment holiday' for the first year of the loan. This means that you only pay interest and do not begin repaying capital until a later date when (hopefully) the nursery is making a profit.

Loans are a good form of finance for long-term assets, or where you know you will need to borrow money for some time, as this offers the business financial stability: provided you are making the loan repayments as required, the loan cannot usually be withdrawn. However, you will be paying interest on the full amount of the outstanding loan whether or not you need the money all the time – hence this is not a good form of finance for fluctuating working capital needs.

Overdraft facility

An overdraft facility is an agreement for the bank to offer you a specified amount of credit on your current account, which you then drawn on (up to the limit) as and when you need it.

You only pay interest on the overdrawn balance, not on the full amount of the facility, which makes this a suitable form of finance for fluctuating cash flow management.

However, the interest rates can be higher than for term loans, and overdrafts are repayable on demand, which means that the bank can (in theory at least) ask you to repay the overdraft immediately at any time. This makes it an unstable form of finance.

Fees and charges

Banks charge arrangement fees for loans and overdrafts, as a set percentage of the facility. The loan arrangement fee is payable once only at the beginning of the loan, whereas the overdraft fee is payable each year on renewal of the facility. The overdraft fee is paid on the full facility, regardless of how much you actually draw down during the year.

Security

Very few banks will offer loans or overdrafts to small businesses, especially to new ones, without some form of security, so you should be prepared to discuss this with your bank. They will be looking for assets you hold which you will agree they can sell to repay the loan or overdraft if the business is unable to meet repayments. Typically these assets will be property or investments. The bank usually deducts a percentage of the valuation to represent the effect of a forced sale. For example, if you had a loan of £20 000, they would expect security over a property worth, say, £25 000 to allow for a reduction in value due to selling the property quickly.

WATCH POINT

You should take legal advice before giving a bank a charge over any of your assets, especially where this is your family home. It is important that you understand fully the implications of a bank charge before entering into such an agreement.

VENTURE CAPITAL

Equity finance can be raised through venture capital companies. It is important to realise that the venture capital investors become shareholders in your business. This means that you do not pay any interest to them but they will have a share in the total profits of your business. They will also, as shareholders, have a greater degree of control and influence over the development of your nursery, so you must be quite satisfied that their values and objectives are consistent with providing a good quality childcare service.

WATCH POINT

Venture capital companies generally seek high returns on their money, which in turn could put you under great pressure to keep costs low or fees high, and generally affect your nursery policies.

As a venture capital company becomes a shareholder in your business, this means that you will have to structure your business as a limited company should you decide to raise finance through this route. Such companies will normally only consider:

■ investments for a minimum of £100 000, which may be more than you need
■ investments which they can seek to sell in around 5 to 7 years.

You therefore need to be able to demonstrate to them that there is an 'exit route', in other words, that your business will have increased in value significantly at the end of the investment period, and that there will be a market for the shares in your company, or that you will be able to buy them back.

For a business comprising one nursery alone, this makes venture capital an unlikely proposition, but if you envisage a network of nurseries, and you expect to be able to buy back the shares or interest from other investors once the business is established, then this might be worth looking at. You will undoubtedly have to demonstrate strong business acumen, as venture capitalists look for a strong management team to achieve the growth they are seeking.

As with all financial matters, you will need good professional advice. You will need to make sure that:

■ your business is valued correctly
■ the venture capitalist does not take too high a stake
■ the business proposition is realistic
■ the fees charged are appropriate.

WATCH POINT

It would be advisable to take independent financial advice, perhaps from your accountant, before selling shares in your business to a venture capital investor.

As an alternative, you might choose to interest your family and friends in supporting your new business financially. This has the advantage of providing equity capital (without the demands of debt) but from people who know and trust you, and who are closer to your business and childcare objectives than an institutional investor. You may be able to raise smaller sums of money through this route, but your friends and family will almost certainly be motivated differently from a venture capitalist – and hence less demanding in terms of the returns they expect – and there will not be pressure to sell the business within a certain time frame.

NON-COMMERCIAL FUNDS

Details of these schemes change from time to time, and in some cases vary locally. Your local Training and Enterprise Council (TEC), Business Link office or Chamber of Commerce should be able to provide you with details, and they may also be able to offer you advice and support with your business planning. Some details of these schemes are also available through banks.

The Government Loan Guarantee Scheme involves borrowing from a bank, but a high proportion of the loan (usually 70% for new businesses, 85% for existing businesses) will be guaranteed by the Government (currently via the Department of Trade and Industry). The scheme applies to new loans only, not to the replacement of existing loans, and there is a limit on the amount which can be borrowed (currently £100 000 for new businesses and £250 000 for existing businesses). As the loan is guaranteed, banks are more willing to consider lending to new businesses without an established track record, but you will, of course, have to convince the bank of the viability of your plans.

Other funds are available from other organisations which aim to help businesses start up, especially where they could not do so by relying on commercial funding. These may be run by local authorities to encourage new businesses to set up in their area, or they may be enterprise funds set up by local or national charities or companies as part of their community giving programme.

GRANTS

Grants represent another possible source of finance, with the added advantage that they do not need to be repaid. However, there are now relatively few sources, with many of the national and local grant-givers having moved to 'soft' loans and away from grants, in order to increase the number of businesses they are able to assist.

Grants are available mainly from:
- the Department of Trade and Industry
- local authorities (usually through their Economic Development Units)
- Training and Enterprise Councils
- the Prince's Youth Business Trust, for those aged under 30 years
- the European Community.

Usually your local authority is the best starting point, especially if you are in an area ear-marked for special funding. You may find that, as soon as you mention childcare, you are pigeon-holed along with other community childcare projects. This may be advantageous, but do persevere in explaining that you are seeking assistance as a business start-up which happens to be based around childcare, otherwise you will miss the grants which are available to businesses generally as opposed to childcare development specifically.

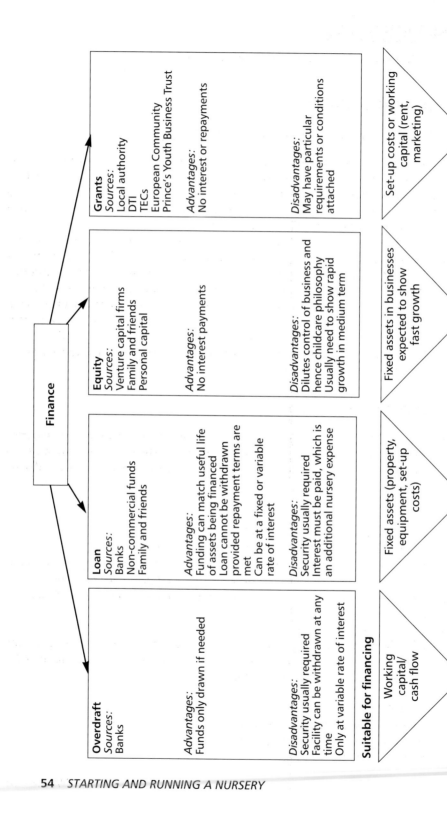

Finance

Overdraft
Sources:
Banks

Advantages:
Funds only drawn if needed

Disadvantages:
Security usually required
Facility can be withdrawn at any time
Only at variable rate of interest

Loan
Sources:
Banks
Non-commercial funds
Family and friends

Advantages:
Funding can match useful life of assets being financed
Loan cannot be withdrawn provided repayment terms are met
Can be at a fixed or variable rate of interest

Disadvantages:
Security usually required
Interest must be paid, which is an additional nursery expense

Equity
Sources:
Venture capital firms
Family and friends
Personal capital

Advantages:
No interest payments

Disadvantages:
Dilutes control of business and hence childcare philosophy
Usually need to show rapid growth in medium term

Grants
Sources:
Local authority
DTI
TECs
European Community
Prince's Youth Business Trust

Advantages:
No interest or repayments

Disadvantages:
May have particular requirements or conditions attached

Suitable for financing

Working capital/cash flow

Fixed assets (property, equipment, set-up costs)

Fixed assets in businesses expected to show fast growth

Set-up costs or working capital (rent, marketing)

Each type of financing has advantages and disadvantages

Grants sometimes have special conditions attached.

Seeking finance

THE IMPORTANCE OF A BUSINESS PLAN

Whichever form of finance you decide to seek, you will need to prepare a business plan which supports your case. This will apply even if you intend seeking support from family or friends; they will want to know why you are borrowing the money, what you will do with it, when and how you will pay it back, and what might cause you to be unable to repay their money.

Your business plan must convince an investor of your nursery's viability, whilst being realistic about the possible risks. Your plan should demonstrate that both you and the financier will receive some income from the nursery, and that the investor's capital will be repaid. It should also represent your credentials, in both childcare and business management, as a person (or team) capable of managing a childcare business. The business plan will also provide a framework against which you can monitor performance and plan for future growth.

You will need to ensure that the document you prepare for investors covers all the information they will be seeking.

QUESTIONS INVESTORS ASK

It is well worth pre-empting all the questions investors may ask. What investors look for and the questions they ask depend on the type of finance you are seeking, but there are some generic questions investors will pose. They fall under six main headings.

What?
- What will you use the money for?
- Is it for set-up capital or for working capital finance?
- Specifically what will you be spending it on? (Give details of premises alterations, equipment lists, salaries of staff pre-opening, initial marketing etc.)
- How have you arrived at your costings? (Builders' estimates? Catalogue prices? Past experience?)
- How will the assets be used to generate income?
- How long will the assets last? (This should be at least as long as the loan/investment that you are seeking, otherwise you will need funding for new assets before you have paid for the first set.)

How much?
- How much will you need to borrow?
- How did you arrive at this figure?
- Why no more and no less?

- What might change the amount you need? (Enrolments not building up? Unforeseen additional costs in premises alterations?)

Why?
- Why do you need to seek external funds?
- Why did you choose this particular funding source? Why is it appropriate for your circumstances?
- Are you putting in any of your own funds? How much?

How?
- How will the money be repaid?
- How will interest payments be met?
- What are the profit projections? (so that the investor can see how you plan to generate income)
- What might change these projections and hence affect the ability to repay?
- What are your cash flow forecasts? (so that the investor can see that you will have the cash to repay)

When?
- When will the funds be needed? (Immediately? On opening the nursery? In installments over several months?)
- When will you repay the loan or investment? Will it be repaid in one lump sum, or in installments? Will you need a capital repayment holiday?
- Will repayment involve the sale of any assets or of the business as a whole?
- Are you offering any security against repayment of a loan? What is this? What value does it have? What might affect the value of this asset?

Who?
- Who will be responsible for repaying the loan?
- Who are you? What qualifications and experience do you have?
- What track record do you have which will satisfy the investor that you are a suitable person in whom to place trust?

RISK AND RETURN

Investing in businesses is all about judging risk and return. Whichever form of finance you opt for, this is what the investor or lender will be trying to weigh up. Will I get my money back? What might prevent me getting my money back? Am I likely to earn a suitable return on my money? What might affect that? Am I comfortable with the risks involved? In your application you will need to provide as much information as possible to help the investor make these judgements, and convince him or her that your nursery will be a good business to support.

APPLYING FOR A GRANT

If you are applying for a grant, you will need to answer a similar set of questions, except that the organisation granting the funds will not be concerned about repayment of the money, but about how, when and to what extent you will meet their criteria for giving the grant. It is worth thinking hard about these, and finding out as much as possible about the grant criteria before applying for grants.

Typically the outcomes a nursery can offer which might fit with grant criteria are:

■ new business start-up
■ economic regeneration
■ job creation
■ opportunities for women
■ development of community services
■ links to training
■ plugging gaps in services (e.g. providing childcare places for babies)
■ supporting pre-school services.

Conclusion

You will almost certainly need at least some financial investment in order to start your nursery. Obtaining funding is essentially a marketing exercise to which it is important to give adequate thought. If you are to persuade investors to finance your nursery, you will need to put effort into convincing them that yours is a venture worth investing in. Then, with a solid financial foundation, you will be able to move forward.

CHECKLIST

Set-up capital needed
■ Initial market research
■ Premises
■ Professional fees (solicitor, accountant, architect)
■ Builders
■ Equipment
■ Bank arrangement fees and charges
■ Printing leaflets, literature, forms etc.
■ Staff recruitment (adverts, forms, postage, phone calls, rent of room to interview)
■ Deposits on services (telephone, gas, electricity)
■ Local authority registration fee

Working capital needed
■ Staff salaries until fee income reaches sufficient level to cover them
■ Bills for heat and light, telephone, rent, rates etc.
■ Weekly nursery expenditure on food, cleaning, hygiene, consumables, additional equipment etc.
■ Advertising and marketing costs
■ Interest and bank charges

CHECKLIST continued

Exploring financing options
- Own resources and security offered
- Bank loans and overdrafts
- Government and enterprise loan schemes
- Venture capital
- Grants
- Family and friends

Arranging finance
- Amount
- Period of loan/investment
- Interest rate
- Arrangement fees and other charges
- Security taken
- Special conditions/criteria

5 BANKING AND CASH MANAGEMENT

You can be as romantic as you please about love ... but you mustn't be romantic about money.

George Bernard Shaw

In this chapter we discuss the type of banking arrangements you will need to establish for your nursery, and suggest how to use banking services. We look at what you need to do to keep track of your money – your payments, receipts and cash balances. We also suggest how to make sure you get the best possible service from your bank, and how to develop a relationship with your bank which is supportive and helpful to your nursery business.

Using banking services

It will be necessary to open a bank account through which to pay your bills, receive fees, and to hold your cash balances. The nursery staff will also require access to cash and cheque payments in order to take responsibility for expenditure incurred directly by the nursery. Decisions need to be made about the type of banking and cash handling arrangements the nursery needs to operate, from which bank to purchase these services, and how to manage the nursery bank accounts and bank relationships.

BANKING ARRANGEMENTS

The way in which you set up your banking arrangements will depend on the legal structure within which you have chosen to operate, the extent to which you are delegating purchasing responsibility to your staff, the degree to which administrative and finance tasks are dealt with by the manager, and the level of sophistication you wish to bring to the financial management of your business.

Every nursery will need, as a minimum:
- a current account through which to make payments by cheque, standing order or direct debit instruction, from which to withdraw cash, and into which to deposit cheques and receive standing order payments

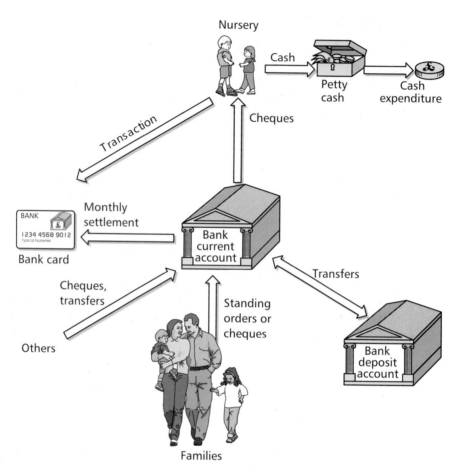

Typical nursery financial transactions

- a facility for nursery staff to withdraw cash in order to pay for nursery purchases, which may include food, cleaning and hygiene materials, consumables, materials for activities, outings, small items of equipment and other essential supplies which are best purchased locally.

In addition the following facilities are useful:

- payments to several recipients through one total payment. This is useful for paying regular creditors to whom you make payments on the same day, or for paying staff salaries. Usually the bank gives you a code for each recipient account, and you quote the amount to be paid to each code. This system eases the financial administration, is a cheaper form of payment than cheque and avoids postage for each cheque.
- a company bank card which enables you and the nursery staff to make purchases without using cash. This acts like a company charge card, and can be used in most retail outlets.

CHOOSING A BANK

It is quite likely that all the high street banks offer the type of banking services your nursery will need, but it would be worth asking a selection of them for their literature to compare the details of the services that are relevant. It is also sensible to compare bank charges. Many of the banks offer introductory packages for new businesses, such as free banking for the first year if you are in credit, or a free gift to help with the start-up of your business.

It is sensible to compare charges when you are choosing a bank

Your choice of bank may be determined by your choice of financier – if you have arranged an overdraft or a loan with a bank you will probably have to bank with them too. When choosing your bank (whether for finance or purely for banking services), it is worth finding a branch of your chosen bank where you are likely to be able to build a good relationship and gain a sympathetic hearing. There are a number of ways to set about making your choice of bank. You may find the following ideas helpful.

Existing banking relationship
Do you have an existing bank relationship? It would be worth talking to the manager of the branch at which you have your personal account as he or she will have known you for some time. An established track record as a good customer who can handle finances sensibly is important to a banking relationship.

Introduction
Can anyone offer you an introduction to a bank and/or branch? Perhaps your accountant or your solicitor would be able to help, or a family member or friend? It usually helps to come to a bank with an introduction, especially if you are seeking finance.

Banks with experience of nurseries

Which banks do other nurseries use? Your local branch of the National Private Day Nurseries Association (NPDNA) might be able to suggest banks which understand the particular requirements of nurseries. Ideally you should find a bank and branch with a manager who knows and understands the childcare sector.

Bank manager who can empathise

Is there a local branch of a bank with a manager who has young children, and hence is likely to be able to identify closely with the success of your nursery, and understand the childcare issues involved in managing your business?

Ideally you should find a bank manager who understands the childcare sector

Local connections

Your local TEC may have connections with local branches of banks which are particularly helpful to new businesses. Your local Chamber of Commerce might also be able to help.

Information in bank literature

Look at the literature supplied by the banks. Some target their services specifically at the small business sector and they may be more suitable than others.

SETTING UP YOUR BANKING FACILITIES

When you open an account with a bank you will need to complete the formalities according to the bank's own procedures. Generally you will need to make an appointment to meet the bank representative in person, complete the application forms, and provide the names and addresses of and personal identification for the key people who will be financially responsible for the nursery (you and any business partners, or the directors if you have set up a company). If you are operating the nursery through a company, you will need to provide the Certificate of Incorporation and the Memorandum and Articles of Association of the company. The bank will run credit checks on the individuals involved, and a Companies House search on the company, if relevant.

The bank should then go through with you the facilities they offer, and help you choose and set up those that are relevant to you. As a minimum you will need to decide on the bank mandate – who may sign cheques and for what amounts. In deciding this you will need to balance control over funds with practical considerations. It would be unwise to allow nursery staff to withdraw large amounts of cash from the bank account, but equally they will need to be able to pay for provisions purchased directly by the nursery (unless you are prepared to do this yourself). Generally you would put restrictions on:

- who can sign a cheque as sole signatory or as joint signatory
- the amount which can be signed on each basis
- who can sign cheques for withdrawing cash, and up to what amount
- who can collect cash from the bank.

If your bank branch is not near your nursery, you will have to arrange for cash collection at a local branch of the bank. Your bank will help you set this up.

Your bank will then issue you with cheque books and paying-in books, and you can start using the account once you have paid funds into it, or once you have an overdraft facility in place.

Keeping track of your money

MAKING PAYMENTS

Most nurseries have three main types of payment they have to make:

- regular weekly, monthly or quarterly payments such as salaries, PAYE/NIC, rent, rates, electricity, gas, telephone and insurance
- purchases which are invoiced as incurred, such as equipment and consumables purchases, some maintenance or employing agency staff
- payments for items which are purchased and paid for directly by the nursery staff, whether in cash, by cheque or with a bank or credit card. These may include food, cleaning and hygiene materials, consumables and items for activities, outings for the children, smaller items of maintenance such as window cleaning or gardening, and stationery.

You will need to work out the easiest, most efficient and most cost effective method of making each type of payment. This involves thinking about practicalities first. Who is authorising the expenditure? Can this be delegated? Can the nursery place orders for items to be invoiced?

It is also worth considering the transaction costs for each type of payment in order to minimise your bank charges. Cash payments are the most expensive, and automatic payments are the cheapest. It is worth trying to automate as many payments as possible, and to avoid paying for items by cash or in small cheques. Automatic payments include direct debits, standing orders, and systems which allow payment of several regular creditors in one payment using a code for each creditor – these need to be set up with your bank.

From an administrative perspective it is helpful to rationalise your main payments so that these are all made on one or two days of the month. For example, you could pay your rent, rates and all your previous month creditors in one automatic payment each month.

RECEIVING MONEY

The main source of income for your nursery will be fees from parents, but you may have other sources of income which you will need to arrange to receive, e.g. grants, money paid by parents for items such as photographs, sweatshirts or outings, and deposits from parents.

The banking arrangements for receiving money will depend largely on how you will ask parents to pay their fees to you. The arrangements will depend on your preferences, and how far in advance parents are able to pay their fees. Most nurseries charge fees one month in advance, but some charge fees weekly and others quarterly. Probably the best arrangement, if you can achieve it, is to have fees paid monthly on the first of each month – or some other date, but with all parents paying on the same day in order to reduce the administration. If you can arrange for parents to pay by standing order you will reduce your administration, reduce the time you spend on invoicing and debt collecting, reduce your bank charges, and improve your cash flow (because fees will be collected automatically when due).

If at all possible you should avoid fees being collected by the nursery staff. This administration reduces the time staff can spend with the children, and makes it harder for you to monitor the collection of fees. You may find that staff are unable to go to the bank regularly (because of nursery duties) so that cheques or cash remain unbanked for some time, therefore reducing your cash flow.

Even if your fees are collected by standing order, you will need to make sure that the nursery manager has a paying-in book, and can pay cheques into the local bank. You will find there are still some cheques to bank, especially if you charge parents a fee for registering a child on the waiting list. Cheques for one-off invoices, e.g. when a child first enrolls at the nursery, or fees for additional days, are also likely.

CASH MANAGEMENT

When starting and managing a new business it is very important to monitor your bank and cash balances, and to keep track of expenditure. In order to do this you will need to maintain full records of income and expenditure. Details of the accounting records needed for a nursery are described in the Chapter 14, but it is worth mentioning in connection with banking and cash management that you will need to maintain records of the expenditure incurred by the nursery, and the cash float maintained.

It is important to monitor bank and cash balances

All direct nursery expenditure should be recorded on a weekly basis by the nursery manager, to be incorporated into the accounting records. As part of the bank reconciliation it is important to check the nursery cheques issued and cheques banked against the bank statement.

There are a number of ways of laying out the nursery expenditure, but generally the forms will need to include:

- a list of items purchased by cash (petty cash expenditure)
- a list of items purchased by bank card – if the nursery has one
- details of all cheques issued by the nursery to third parties
- details of all cheques cashed by the nursery
- details of any cheques banked by the nursery, with paying-in slip references
- a reconciliation of the cash balance in the petty cash box to the balance brought forward, less expenditure plus cheques cashed by the nursery.

When designing your forms you will need to make sure that you include all the information you need in a lay-out which is clear and easy to complete. It is sensible to include an explanation as to how to complete the form.

Managing your banking relationship

It is well worth maintaining a good relationship with your bank, especially if you have borrowed money from the bank. Equally, there is no need to be intimidated by your bank, and you should feel able to make valid complaints if the service does not meet your requirements, or if you find errors or overcharging.

Like all good relationships, your relationship with your bank needs to be two way, and to be based on good communication. You may find more detailed suggestions in other texts on how to manage a small business relationship with a bank, but the following are suggestions which we have found useful and which are especially applicable to a nursery.

Contractual relationship

Make sure you know the basis of the contractual relationship between you and your bank, whether this is one of borrower/lender or of provider of services/customer. Make sure you are happy with the terms and conditions, and if you are not, take this up with the bank manager.

Personal contact

Get to know who is the person with main responsibility for your account, arrange to meet them and encourage them to visit your nursery. Use this as an opportunity to explain how your business works, what your objectives are and how the business dynamics operate. Try to explain anything about a nursery which might be different from other businesses. For example, explain why you cannot necessarily maintain a low cost base while enrolments build up because you have to provide a core staff team on opening, or clarify why you cannot enroll more babies even though you have a waiting list for babies and vacancies for older children.

Communicate progress

Keep the bank up-to-date on progress, and tell them about your successes as well as the difficulties. This helps the bank build up confidence in you. You might do this by sending the monthly or quarterly management accounts with a short report, or by occasionally ringing your bank manager. You might discuss with your bank how they like to monitor progress.

Seek help early

If you think you might need additional help, it is usually sensible not to delay talking to your bank. They may be able to help prevent any difficult financial situations arising. Be honest but constructive, but also remember that it is generally easier to borrow money from the bank before you actually need it rather than when you are desperate – so it is wise to think ahead and forecast accordingly.

Check charges

Always check your bank charges and interest charges. The banks are not always right. Do not be afraid of querying charges and asking them to rectify errors.

Conclusion

Banking arrangements which work well are important for the smooth running of your nursery. By putting time into setting this up, you will make sure that the nursery minimises time spent on administration, and can make purchases as and when needed. Your bank should be able to help you set up and use the banking services, and should offer support and advice as part of a supportive bank/customer relationship.

CHECKLIST

Banking services
- Current account
- Access to cash
- Bank card
- Automatic payments

Choosing a bank
- Services offered
- Terms and charges
- Convenience
- Reputation
- Existing banking relationship
- Introduction
- Knowledge of childcare sector
- Local networks

Setting up banking facilities
- Cheque signatories
- Arrangements for withdrawing cash

Payments
- Regular
- Nursery
- Nursery expenditure forms
- Timing
- Method

Receipts
- Method and frequency of invoicing and receiving payments
- Nursery paying-in book

Bank relationships
- Contractual relationship
- Initial meeting
- Regular updates and visits
- Planning banking needs
- Check charges and interest

6 *PREMISES DESIGN*

> **What this chapter covers:**
> - **Complying with regulations**
> - **The arrangement of space within the premises**
> - **Seeking good advice**
> - **General design principles**
> - **Decoration and soft furnishings**
> - **Health and safety considerations**
> - **Children's areas**
> - **Adult areas**
> - **The building process**

A house is a living machine.

Le Corbusier

The purpose of this chapter is to outline the steps involved in making premises suitable for nursery use. It includes reference to the range of legalities and practicalities which have to be negotiated.

In the process of setting up a nursery, the choice of premises and the design of the nursery are early matters for resolution. The layout, appearance and amenities will impact significantly on staff performance and parental perceptions. They also have direct implications for quality issues and the quality of life for the children. It is important to get the nursery design right. In fact, the choice of location for the nursery should be influenced initially by the design possibilities of the site.

Complying with regulations

It is prudent to make early contact with the appropriate statutory authorities before proceeding to finalise the design plans and arrangements for building work. Approval must be sought from the registration officer, environmental health officer, fire officer and the district surveyor. Meeting the requirements and obtaining the necessary approval can be time consuming and costly. It is important to get everything right in the first instance in order to avoid potentially ruinous delays or refusals. Without the necessary approval the nursery cannot operate.

REGISTRATION

Registration, usually carried out via the local authority Registration and Inspection Unit, is necessary to allow the nursery to open. Registration officers will focus initially on the suitability of the premises for the ages and numbers of children proposed as well as on health and safety matters and other statutory requirements.

ENVIRONMENTAL HEALTH

Environmental health requirements must be met. These focus on the proximity of food service areas to toilets, ventilation, hygienic floor and wall surfaces, hygienic and safe design of kitchens and other food areas, toilets, nappy changing areas and so on.

FIRE

The fire officer's approval must be sought and requirements met. The focus will be on site access for fire and emergency services, exit routes from the premises, locks and signs, selection and maintenance of fire appliances, alarm systems and emergency lighting, suitability of internal doors, flammability of materials being used and methods of containing fire within areas of the building.

DISTRICT SURVEYOR

The district surveyor has to be notified and consulted about any new building or conversion work. Particular attention must be paid to structural supports, drains, electricity supply, related fire matters and general compliance with established building codes.

The arrangement of space within the premises

It is crucial to use the space available to its best advantage to support the operational plan. This applies equally to both indoor and outdoor space. Whilst each nursery site will present its own challenges and possibilities, there are some general points which illustrate the issues involved.

DISTANCES AND SERVICES

Adult:child ratios are likely to be over-stretched if nappy change areas, toilets, milk kitchens and children's coat pegs are too far away from the area in which the children are active. Their lack of proximity will regularly distance staff from the larger group of children and other staff, thus putting undue strain on ratios and working against standards by impacting negatively on the nursery programme.

ADEQUATE LARGE SPACES

An absence of large rooms can inhibit the use of larger play equipment such as soft play mattresses, ball ponds, big building blocks and climbing frames. This works against the provision of a well-rounded programme, and limits opportunities for the children.

SUPPORT FOR LEARNING

In order for the children to make real choices and to use initiative there has to be sufficient space in the children's activity areas to hold a full range of equipment and storage furniture. Free floor space is also important to support more than one activity taking place at the same time.

CORRIDORS

Proper corridors are needed so that all parts of the nursery are individually accessible without causing disruption to the children's activities.

WALLS AND CORNERS

Rooms which are broken up by many doors and windows limit the flexibility of use and work against provision of home corners, book corners, child-accessible storage units, workshop areas, etc., which should focus children's attention for learning purposes.

ACCESS FOR OUTDOOR ACTIVITIES

Limited access to the outdoor space, through factors such as location of exits, or width of doors, or distance from the children's coat pegs can inhibit appropriate use of the gardens and other outdoor areas, and may deprive the children of fresh air. Limited access prevents an easy flow between indoor and outdoor learning.

OUTDOOR SECURITY

Secure boundaries, especially for outdoor spaces, are necessary to prevent intrusions from strangers or unsupervised exits by children. However, there may be a requirement to facilitate a fire exit route or access by the emergency services.

OUTDOOR AMENITIES

The location of trees, gradients, shelter from the sun and wind, and ground conditions will dictate the arrangement of the outdoor space. A range of surfaces, e.g. hard surfaces, soft play areas and grass, must be provided in order to accommodate a variety of activities for the varying age groups as well as the changes in weather.

GARDEN PLANNING CHART		
Nursery activities Babies Toddlers Older children Physical Natural world Creative Imaginative Summer Winter	**Facilities needed**	**Ideal location**
Time of day Early morning Mid-morning Mid-day Early afternoon Late afternoon	**Areas in shade**	**Areas in the sun**
Surfaces/gradients Grass Planting area Hard surface Safety surface Steep incline Flat area	**Intended use**	**Location**
Planting and landscaping Existing features Spring flowering Summer gardening Winter colour Attractive to birds Attractive to insects	**Use**	**Location**
Maintenance Surfaces Fixed equipment Trees Grass Plants	**Type needed**	**Season**
Existing garden site	**Initial development**	**Mature plan**

Example of a garden planning chart

Seeking good advice

Whether you are undertaking a new build or carrying out conversion or adaptation work to existing premises, the nursery will benefit from the services of experienced advisers, preferably those who know something about children and childcare.

ARCHITECT

At the very least, it is likely that the services of an architect will be needed to prepare the basic drawings which will have to be submitted to the local council with the planning application. The architect will also be particularly helpful in managing the conflicts between statutory regulations and the best use of space in the nursery. An architect can advise on structural matters (sometimes alongside a structural engineer), heating systems, how to maintain required room temperatures and control the hot water temperatures, suitable doors and door handles, safety glass, ventilation, colour schemes, etc. It will be particularly beneficial to achieving a satisfactory result to have the architect write up detailed specifications and provide drawings for use by the builders. Additional guidance on tendering, selecting a builder, agreeing a contract, arranging insurance during the building work and offering support if difficulties arise, are all invaluable architects' services.

DESIGNER

There are some specialist nursery designers who cover a very wide range of services. In some circumstances they may be able to replace the architects. However, it is more usual for such designers to focus on issues such as colour schemes, soft furnishings, murals and garden design. If the budget allows for this design work then the nursery is likely to be visually attractive with a unique image.

PRACTITIONER

Do not overlook the value of consulting an experienced nursery worker when beginning to design the nursery. Someone who is imaginative and understands the operation of a nursery will be able to visualise the way the premises will be used and anticipate possible difficulties for which solutions can be planned. They can work with the architects to choose between options and will know what is practical and desirable. Finding this nursery worker may not be easy and will, of course, incur an additional cost, but their involvement will, in the long-term, amply repay the time and expense of seeking their advice.

General design principles

Good design is about visually attractive practical efficiency. Well-planned pleasant facilities will serve the nursery well. Reserving some of the budget for small items of additional work, which will invariably be recognised once the nursery is up and running, is a sensible plan. This also allows the staff and the children to make some input to the design of their environment.

FLEXIBILITY

Whilst special built-in play features may be appealing at first, they are all too frequently found to be impractical when the nursery is in operation. This may be one area of the design in which it is necessary to restrain an enthusiastic architect or designer.

Beware of seemingly clever or faddish ideas. This applies especially to wallpaper and curtains which can be costly and eventually hard to maintain.

Flexibility in how the nursery rooms can be used is a valuable asset. Once the nursery is functioning new initiatives will be identified by staff and children and enrolment patterns will change. Being responsive to new demands may include altering the way spaces in the nursery are used. The more flexibility possible, the more the nursery programme can be enriched, and children accommodated.

USER PERSPECTIVE

Reflecting the children's perspective on the nursery design is a must at all stages. Whilst it is not possible to engage a child as an adviser, it is possible to observe children in other nurseries and to draw sensitive conclusions about how they use space and what spaces are especially relevant to the care and learning programmes. Textbooks and professional advisors can provide guidance on safety aspects.

It is important for planners to try to imagine real children in the nursery. The ethos of child-centred provision is well illustrated by a charming anecdote about an architect and nursery owner crawling around the nursery site on hands and knees to see the environment as children would.

Consideration of the perspective of the adults using the nursery is also important. Staff have specific job functions to perform which may at times require a secure, quiet space or a degree of isolation in order to protect the children. Parents need space to gather and will seek a degree of privacy when they want to discuss their children or financial arrangements. Role playing a day in the lives of a nursery cook, manager, child care worker and parent, should provoke a greater understanding of what the adults' requirements will be for your proposed premises.

Decoration and soft furnishings

Ambience is largely created by the choice of furnishings, colours, patterns and textures used in the decoration of premises. The nursery ambience should be cheerful, visually appealing, harmonious and appropriate to the ages of the children. This does not necessarily have to involve a lot of expense. Sensitive planning will do the trick!

CONSIDERING COLOUR	
Warm colours	**Cool colours**
yellow orange red appear to advance forward	green blue violet appear to move away from the eye
Dark colours	**Light colours**
are dramatic at night attract attention	look best in the daytime provide good backgrounds to displays
Contrasting colour schemes	**Complementary and monochromatic schemes**
are visually stimulating but can create restless tension	offer subtle harmony but too much can be visually tiring

Considering colour chart

As with all aspects of the nursery, the decor should take account of the child's perspective. So you should consider the design and colour of the skirting boards, the area of wall below the level of the dado, the ceilings above the nappy change and sleep areas, the location of mirrors and so on, including even the home corner furnishings and the dressing up facilities.

COLOUR

Colour is recognised as having an affect on emotions and behaviour; it can differentiate boundaries between spaces and is also used to highlight hazards. You would be sensible to consider the various implications of colour theory when planning your nursery decor. A good starting point is to choose a general colour pallet which suits the natural light available. For example, cool, gloomy rooms need warm colours. Dark areas need light and bright colours. White and pastels open up areas and enhance the feeling of spaciousness.

The patterns and colours used by manufacturers in cots, tables, play equipment, etc. will need to be taken into account when you are choosing colours and fabrics. It should not be too difficult to find items which are harmonious. Similarly suppliers of ready-made kitchen units, doors and door furniture offer some choice. However, beware of 'safe' colours, such as beige and naturally stained woods. They may seem to be practical, from the adult point of view, but they do not offer much attractiveness to children and can cast an air of gloom in a nursery.

COMFORT

Cushions, small rugs and curtains make as great an impact as wall colours. They also have a crucial role in supporting the care and learning programmes for the children. A special area can be created and then easily moved to a new location, as activity needs dictate. Comfortable and quiet areas can be created to encourage reading for pleasure. A rug and some cushions can provide a safe haven at the end of a long day. Babies can be nestled in sag bags, or propped up to play on a rug and protected by a buffer of cushions.

Finally do not forget the ambience in the adult areas. Colour and style, etc. should echo that of the children's areas. Staff need comfortable and pleasant surroundings in the staff room. The reception area, office and food preparation rooms are as much a part of the nursery as the children's play areas. The whole nursery should 'work' aesthetically.

Health and safety considerations

Safety, security and hygiene deserve a lot of attention. They will also take up a large share of the budget. However, it is unarguably worthwhile to invest in a safe environment.

- Door knobs, coat pegs and similar protuberances should be installed at suitable heights to avoid injuries to children's eyes and heads. Some items, e.g. catches on external doors, may need to be placed at very high levels, above normal adult levels, to prevent children from using them.
- Internal doors should have viewing panels both at adult height and at child height so the children can see and be seen.
- • Low surface temperature radiators reduce the likelihood of burns, and eliminate the need for dust catching radiator guards. Hot pipes which are exposed will need to be guarded or boxed in.
- Visual surveillance of all entrances, and all nooks and corners should be planned. Viewing panels may be inserted in walls. Mirrors may be fixed to reflect hidden areas. Fences and gates should be fitted to prevent uninvited access. Careful consideration should be given to the security of external doors.
- Exterior lights on the building, in the outdoor space and in parking areas will not only prevent accidents, deter burglars and give the staff working on the late shift a sense of personal safety, but will also increase the opportunities for children to play outside on dark winter afternoons.
- Fixed play equipment in outdoor spaces should be surrounded by an impact absorbing surface which should extend 1.5-2.0 m beyond the edge of the equipment. Commercially applied surfaces need to comply with British Standard specifications.
- Industrial quality stainless steel work tops are easy to keep clean, durable and contain no patterns or crevices to harbour germs.

Children's areas

Children's activity and rest areas should be well planned. The importance of flexibility has already been mentioned. The design also should reflect the need for a variety of environments to support the full range of activities and facilities required for all children, whatever their age. It is particularly important that for the over-threes there is a generous amount of space to allow all equipment to be accessible so that children can use their initiative and make choices about activities, tools, materials, etc.

- Under floor heating is advantageous because it creates a warm setting for children's activities, particularly for crawling babies and early toddlers.
- Acoustic vinyl flooring can reduce noise levels and offset other poor acoustics in the nursery.
- Windows should be at a level suitable for all children to be able to see outside. However, safety bars will be needed to prevent falls.
- Lighting should be bright enough to sustain activities even when it is late in the day. Dimmer switches can be useful for creating subdued light suitable for quiet activities or resting. The additional use of some moveable 'task lighting' is useful for reading stories or close work.
- A low-level changing table, big enough to hold even the older children, will facilitate changing the children. It must be high enough to prevent the need for adults to bend and stretch too much, but it must be low enough so that children can be helped to climb onto it thus avoiding extra back strain and lifting for the staff.

A raised bed will help children to enjoy gardening in all seasons

- There should be at least two nappy changing tables for every eight or nine babies in the nursery. Not only is it likely that several babies will need changing at the same time, but also there will be less disruption to the daily routine if changing can be carried out with the minimum of waiting time.
- An outdoor water tap sited near a small drain will facilitate children's gardening, water play and summer pool activities.
- A raised planting bed in a sunny location in the garden will help children to enjoy gardening in all seasons.

Adult areas

Adult areas and other facilities for staff and parents merit due consideration and will repay any investment through promoting good practices and positive relationships. The boost to professional self confidence, resulting from good facilities, will motivate and assist staff in their work. Parents will feel more welcome and better informed if the facilities reflect a recognition of their needs.

- White boards as well as notice boards fixed in key positions by all telephones, and in the staff room, the kitchen and the office, will support communications between staff, across shift patterns.
- Intercoms and similar devices are easily installed and ensure that messages can be relayed or additional assistance summoned from other parts of the nursery.
- A shelf or writing surface adjacent to each telephone will help to support the taking of written messages, detailed enquiries from prospective parents and the fixing of appointments or outings for the children.
- Adjustable shelving in the toilet, nappy changing and activity areas, office and staff room will provide inexpensive flexible storage. This means bulk purchases, children's clothes, paint and paper, toys, record books and reference material can be readily available where they are needed, and moved to new locations as required.
- A welcoming reception area for parents, with access to information about events, menus, outings etc., will help them to feel valued and involved.
- Restful, comfortably furnished staff facilities will help to mitigate some of the stress of nursery life. A shower, a good makeup mirror and flexible lighting will be appreciated by the staff.

The building process

The choices made, the number of advisers consulted and the standard of finishes commissioned will all be dictated by the nursery's budget and business plan. Nevertheless the building process will be roughly the same in all cases. It is important that the process is understood and followed, because short cuts can create unsatisfactory results. The building process should include:

- initial assessment of the feasibility and costs

- initial reviews of requirements by regulatory officers
- planning application and initial architectural drawings
- design brief for architect
- official approvals (ongoing at various stages)
- written building specification and architectural drawings
- tendering process for selection of builders
- negotiation of contract price, time scale, variations, insurance
- liaison with site manager for building works
- problem solving, final details, snagging lists
- staged payments to builders (ongoing at various stages)
- development of a building manual to locate stopcocks, paint matching etc.
- issuing of certificates for fire, damp proofing, completed building etc.
- arrangement of service contracts for boiler, fire appliances, security alarms etc.

Conclusion

Premises are a major investment and they have to comply with a number of requirements. Organising the arrangements for the premises can be a lengthy process. It is important to choose wisely, to follow the advice of sound advisers and to target expenditure. This should facilitate the creation of the most practical, flexible and pleasant environment possible. It should not be forgotten that the premises are of major significance in how the nursery programme will function and in the maintenance of quality standards.

In addition to the relevant local authority officers, and a qualified architect, advice can be obtained from local libraries and the usual published sources. Some design briefs are available from organisations such as the Daycare Trust and The Stationery Office (formerly HMSO).

There are a wealth of ideas to incorporate into the design of nursery premises. Your advisers will each have suggestions to make. You will observe a range of possibilities on visits to other nurseries. The shape of your premises and the choices you have made for your childcare programme will also highlight limitations and opportunities.

CHECKLIST

Approvals
- Registration
- Environmental health
- Fire
- District surveyor

Advice and process
- Architect
- Experienced early years worker

CHECKLIST continued

- Child's perspective
- Approvals
- Layout and design
- Drawings and specifications
- Building and decorating

Indoor space

- Arrangement of areas and facilities
- Flexibility of use
- Health and safety matters
- Decoration and soft furnishings
- Children's areas
- Babies, toddlers, older children
- Storage for large and small equipment
- Storage for bulk art supplies and special equipment
- Active, quiet, messy, group spaces
- Sleeping space
- Toilet and nappy change areas
- Food preparation areas
- Staff and parent facilities
- Rest, refreshment and personal hygiene facilities
- Storage for food, hygiene supplies, cleaning materials
- Display and information space for children, staff, parents
- Storage for pushchairs (during the day)

Outdoor space

- Arrangement of areas and surfaces
- Boisterous groups, quiet and natural world areas
- Additional facilities, shelter, access to water
- Health and safety matters
- Security measures
- Landscaping and features
- Storage of outdoor play equipment and maintenance equipment

PART B
Focusing on Children

The chapters in this section have been linked together and symbolically placed in the middle of the book because they reflect the core activities of running a nursery. The functioning of the staff team and the organisation of the day-to-day nursery management impact directly on the childcare and learning programmes. Whatever the management arrangements, the focus is ultimately on the children.

The subjects of this central section of the book are directly influenced by issues covered in Getting Started, the first section of the book. For example, the information about local needs gained from market research, and the spatial or design parameters of the premises influence the enrolment numbers, child age profiles and type of learning programme offered. In a parallel way, Focusing on Children impacts on a number of the issues in the Managing for Success section of the book. The qualifications of staff to be recruited, the style of interactions with parents and the quality standards set for the nursery, exemplify aspects of general management which are determined by decisions made about the child-care and learning programmes.

7 THE STAFF TEAM

What this chapter covers:
- **The staff profile**
- **Shift working**
- **Qualifications and qualities of team members**
- **The manager's role**
- **Management styles and structures**
- **Staff communications**
- **Staff development and training**

Provide the climate and proper nourishment and let people grow themselves. They'll amaze you.

Robert Townsend

This chapter is intended to raise issues about staffing requirements and staff management techniques. It is a basic outline of matters to be dealt with, but includes some reference to more specific aspects of arrangements for staff which are sometimes overlooked.

As the quality of nursery provision depends to such a large extent on the nature of the adult–child interactions, staff management and team issues are areas which deserve particular consideration.

The staff profile

The overall staffing plan should be based on how many staff will be required when the nursery reaches its full enrolment. This will facilitate your identification of basic management structures, the seniorities to be established, and the core group of staff needed to see the nursery through from start-up to maturity. The full team is likely to include: manager, deputy, senior nursery officer, nursery officers, nursery assistants, cook and cleaner. In large nurseries or stand-alone establishments the staff team may also include an administrative secretary or accounts assistant, and a domestic assistant.

NUMBER OF STAFF NEEDED

In terms of the exact number of nursery officers and assistants to employ, you will have to take into account a number of factors. These include the layout of the premises, the ages and numbers of children, the percentage of qualified staff and the adult:child ratios which must be maintained to comply with registration requirements, as well as the hours the nursery is open and the number of hours which staff work each day. The guiding principles are that, throughout the nursery opening hours children should always be fully supervised. The bottom line reasoning for this is the safety of the children. Essentially, there should never be less than two experienced workers on duty with a group of children. This applies no matter how small the group of children, nor how close another pair of workers. For example, if there is a fire, sufficient staff are needed to carry the babies to safety and to evacuate all the other children. Often emergencies, such as sickness, or interruptions, such as the arrival of a parent, will demand the attention of one member of staff. Without a second member of staff, as back up, the children can be in danger.

LIMIT TO WORKING HOURS

It is best if staff work no more than 8 or 9 hours per day. Nurseries which demand longer working hours, however many breaks are offered, end up with staff who are perpetually sick or tired, have a high staff turnover and limited recruitment options in competition with better employers. This is certainly a long enough day, given the physical and emotional demands of the job and the level of need of children away from home. What is ultimately best for the children should be the guiding principle.

Shift working

Given that so many nurseries are open for about 10 or 11 hours each day, shift working becomes a necessity. Arranging shifts can sound fairly straightforward, but in fact, it is a complicated matter to meet all the criteria necessary for running a safe and responsive nursery programme.

ADEQUATE STAFF COVER

Either the manager or the deputy or the senior nursery officer need to be available at the beginning and end of each day. They have to talk to parents and visitors, deal with any difficulties and cover for any emergencies or staff absences at short notice.

Additionally, the senior staff members who care for the babies need to be on duty at both ends of the day for continuity and liaison with parents. Someone has to be available to sterilise and make up the babies' bottles, ready to meet their demands. Sufficient experienced staff have to be available to all children and parents to help with greeting, settling in and getting the day's activities off to a good start. There also need to be sufficient experienced staff to provide a high level of support when children are tired at the end of the day and to inform parents about the day's events. Inexperienced or trainee staff and students cannot be left alone in charge.

Operating a three- or four-shift system (early, early middle, late middle, late) should help to bridge the gaps in the day. Using some fixed shifts may suit part time/short hours staff who can work at the beginning and end of the day, when you may need them most. An example of a daily shift pattern is given overleaf.

ADDED BENEFITS

When examining the shift patterns and staff profile, it may seem that the nursery is over-staffed in the middle of the day. However, there are important uses for the 'overlap' periods and functions for the staff team to perform, such as:

■ staff lunch breaks and time for urgent errands
■ shopping to purchase items for a special activity
■ research or arrangements for external resources for an outing or activity
■ special work with an individual child or a small group
■ observations and assessment of children
■ staff appraisals and probationary interviews
■ supervision of students on work placement in the nursery.

A FAIR AND CONSIDERATE SYSTEM

The staff team will undoubtedly view arrangements for shifts as highly important. If shift patterns are not managed properly, staff will come to feel dissatisfaction or disquiet. It is important to be fair to everyone. So, for example, over a period of several weeks of the rotation of shifts, everyone should have the opportunity to work an early shift on a Friday and a late shift on a Monday. Whether shifts change daily or weekly could be agreed within the staff team, because there are views and views!

Qualifications and qualities of team members

The experience and qualifications required for childcare staff will be largely determined by the local authority registration regulations and by the philosophy or ethos you wish to adopt in the nursery. Obviously, qualifications such as the CACHE Diploma in Nursery Nursing (formerly the NNEB), the BTEC Diploma in Nursery Nursing and the NVQ Level III in Childcare and Education are the main qualifications to seek. Financial constraints will also affect recruitment choices.

You may be able to have more flexibility if you can benefit from any of the government employment schemes. It is worth investigating what is on offer via your local Training and Enterprise Council (TEC).

Nevertheless, you should aim to appoint as many fully qualified and appropriately experienced people as possible. Your responsibility to the children and their parents dictates this. Parents have a right to expect a high level of competence from the individuals caring for their children. Registration will require that 50% of the staff have a nationally recognised qualification.

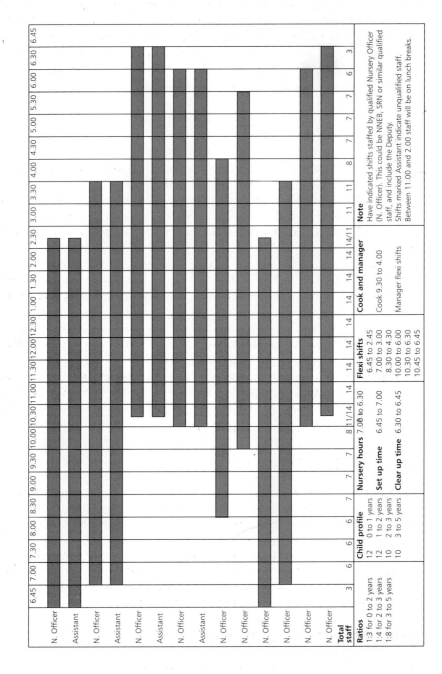

The time scale across the top reads: 6.45 | 7.00 | 7.30 | 8.00 | 8.30 | 9.00 | 9.30 | 10.00 | 10.30 | 11.00 | 11.30 | 12.00 | 12.30 | 1.00 | 1.30 | 2.00 | 2.30 | 3.00 | 3.30 | 4.00 | 4.30 | 5.00 | 5.30 | 6.00 | 6.30 | 6.45

Staff rows (top to bottom): N. Officer, Assistant, N. Officer, Assistant, N. Officer, Assistant, N. Officer, Assistant, N. Officer, N. Officer, N. Officer, N. Officer, N. Officer, N. Officer

| Total staff | 3 | 6 | 6 | 6 | 7 | 6 | 7 | 7 | 8/11/14 | 14 | 14 | 14 | 14 | 14 | 14/11 | 11 | 11 | 8 | 7 | 7 | 7 | 6 | 3 |

Ratios	Child profile	Nursery hours 7.00 to 6.30	Flexi shifts	Cook and manager
1:3 for 0 to 2 years	12 0 to 1 years	Set up time 6.45 to 7.00	6.45 to 2.45	Cook 9.30 to 4.00
1:4 for 2 to 3 years	12 1 to 2 years	Clear up time 6.30 to 6.45	7.00 to 3.00	Manager flexi shifts
1:8 for 3 to 5 years	10 2 to 3 years		8.30 to 4.30	
	10 3 to 5 years		10.00 to 6.00	
			10.30 to 6.30	
			10.45 to 6.45	

Note
Have indicated shifts staffed by qualified Nursery Officer (N. Officer). This could be NNEB, SRN or similar qualified staff, and include the Deputy.
Shifts marked Assistant indicate unqualified staff.
Between 11.00 and 2.00 staff will be on lunch breaks.

Example of a daily shift pattern

Alongside the qualifications and experience required of staff, consideration has to be given to personal qualities. Clearly the outcomes for children are bound to be better if the staff team is a responsive and intelligent one. The ability to show initiative, be self reliant and demonstrate good interpersonal skills are significantly desirable qualities. Standards of spoken English and general literacy (needed to set examples for children and to keep observation/assessment records) will have an impact on quality. Above all else, members of staff must genuinely like and understand children.

The manager's role

The manager holds a pivotal role in fostering the appropriate ethos in the nursery and ensuring good outcomes for the children enrolled. The manager must be able to build and lead the staff team and cope with day-to-day management issues. The manager must also act as the public face of the nursery, dealing with prospective parents, professional visitors, other service providers and parents of the children already enrolled.

The manager may or may not also be the owner of the nursery. To a large extent, the decision on this will be determined by statutory requirements. For registration purposes, the manager has to qualify as the Fit Person under the Children Act Regulations. This includes meeting the required level of professional early years qualifications and having about 5 years of childcare/nursery experience. The Fit Person also has to be competent to ensure that all the legal bottom lines on learning, care, safety and equality are being met.

Finding a qualified and experienced nursery manager, who has the disposition, leadership qualities, personal maturity, sensitivity, knowledge of childcare and range of skills to meet all the requirements of the job, is not easy. A good manager is a rare gem!

MANAGEMENT FUNCTIONS

All of the theories and advice from the well-known management gurus apply to nurseries, though they do need some interpretation and the nursery manager may have to think about the applications. However, regarding nursery management as a sort of special soft option which focuses only on the product (children), diminishes the true role of the manager. In terms of making things happen in the nursery, the manager has to have the authority, competence and time to oversee the running of the nursery in a way which is akin to playing a multi-layer chess game. The manager has a number of key functions.

Quality control and policy implementation
This is significantly based on:
■ clear vision of the ethos and nursery objectives
■ knowledge of all the children as individuals, their development and their relationships

- awareness of the daily routine and the organisation of the activities for the children
- knowledge of changing legal and professional frameworks and the implications of research
- commitment to and understanding of equality issues
- identification of gaps, weaknesses and strengths in the nursery programme
- regular monitoring, problem solving and trouble shooting.

Control of resources
This has to be achieved through:
- prioritising objectives and obligations before taking action
- using time management strategies and maximising the best use of staff time
- making imaginative use of the premises spaces
- understanding and managing budgets and making adjustments as necessary
- matching children's needs with staff skills and equipment selection.

Communications and planning
These are best facilitated by structuring:
- time to be available, to listen and to take action when necessary
- systems for formulating long-term, weekly and daily plans
- prearranged and regular staff meetings and team briefing sessions
- ongoing contact with all parents and events planned especially for parents
- distribution of up-to-date literature on policies and practices for parents and staff
- an approach to showing the nursery to prospective parents and other visitors.

Staff support and performance management
These are appropriately achieved through:
- induction days and probationary periods, with regular reviews, for new staff
- regular observation, interaction, discussion and feedback with each member of staff
- identification of individual skills and team relationships
- annual, interactive, appraisal interviews with each member of staff
- exhibiting action-centred leadership and acting as a trainer
- exemplifying the company culture and nursery ethos, leading by example.

General administration
This has to be based on:
- methodical record-keeping about children, staff, daily events and exceptional events
- simple systems for financial and personnel matters to aid decision making
- use of suitable forms to expedite most matters and meet legal obligations
- access to and control of money and banking services for the nursery
- ensuring that the required supplies and equipment are in place when needed
- ensuring that the premises are in good condition and that all services are functioning properly.

Running the nursery is akin to playing a multi-layer chess game

Management styles and structures

To achieve quality in childcare services an appropriate management infrastructure, which positively influences staff performance, must be in place. Without a suitable working environment and proper management support, even the most imaginative and dedicated carers will be demotivated or confused. For young, inexperienced or untrained carers, it will be almost impossible for them to reach their full potential and to learn to work in ways which will enrich children.

ACTION MANAGEMENT

The manager who spends a substantial part of every day in the nursery working with the children, alongside the other staff, will inevitably have a more realistic grasp of the quality of the programme for children than the manager who is office based. Day-to-day involvement will also facilitate an understanding of the frustrations and difficulties faced by the staff team and will enhance all aspects of team leadership and staff management. More pragmatic reasons for the manager to be in the nursery include providing cover for staff who are working with a very small group of children, releasing staff for non-contact time to work on child records, observations, etc. and creating time for members of staff to carry out some delegated duties such as arranging outings, placing equipment orders, or carrying out health and safety inspections.

STAFF PARTICIPATION

The overall quality of the nursery will benefit if staff have a shared sense of purpose and operate as a confident, motivated team. Women working in nurseries will respond positively to being treated with respect; they seek and deserve to be regarded as more than 'the girls'! The effective management structure allows for involving staff in aspects of management, structuring opportunities for participation in policy development, planning and decision-making, and delegating some senior responsibilities. An added bonus of this system of offering individual opportunities and stretching the skills of staff is that it increases the likelihood of internal promotion. Being able to fill senior staff vacancies, as they arise, from within the existing team is good for maintaining stability in the nursery service.

Staff communications

A strong organisational commitment to good internal communications is essential. Given the very busy nature of nursery life the communications strategy has to be imaginative and to make use of all possibilities. The importance placed on good communications should be made clear to all nursery staff through their contracts, their job descriptions, the induction process and throughout the nursery policies.

STAFF MEETINGS

Staff meetings are a key part of the communication and management process. They must bring all members of staff together at the same time. A minimum of one staff meeting per month is needed and inevitably the meetings will have to be held outside nursery hours, probably on weekday evenings. Meeting dates should be arranged well in advance, perhaps on an annual basis, so that there is sufficient time for everyone to plan to be available on these dates. All members of staff should be expected to attend.

However, it does need to be appreciated that for some of the team it will be a real inconvenience to stay on for an evening, or to return to the nursery when they have worked an early shift. To be fair, everyone should either be paid for their time spent in attending the staff meetings or should be allowed time off in lieu. Members of staff who are working parents may have additional childcare costs to meet and you will have to consider what to do about this.

Formal meetings for the whole team
The use of a pre-planned written agenda will help to keep things on course. One way to encourage full participation in the meetings, and to support good communications, is to circulate a draft agenda several days in advance of the meeting. This will allow all members of staff to contribute to the list of items to be discussed as well as to think about their questions and contributions in advance. The agenda and discussions should be expected to encompass all aspects of the running of the nursery and the planning of the programme for the children.

Minutes of what was agreed at the meeting, who is to be responsible for any follow-up action, and who was present are useful to ensure that the meetings are not just a talking shop. Minutes also provide important information for quality monitoring, other management purposes and OFSTED inspections. It is wise to keep the agendas and minutes in a designated place so that everyone has access to them and can refresh their memories as necessary.

Informal meetings for some staff

More informal discussions are likely to be appropriate if small groups of staff have a need to meet. For example, a meeting may be held to plan for a forthcoming nursery event or festival, or to consider the needs of children of a particular age group or to fine tune a particular part of the learning programme. Such meetings are essential to the running of the nursery, but they can usually be fitted into the middle of the day when other staff are available to cover. Despite the informality, there should be a plan for the meeting; someone should be designated as 'chair' and someone else asked to make notes for future reference.

TEAM BRIEFING

Team briefing is a technique which is often used in business settings to ensure that workers regularly receive up-to-date information, from their manager or supervisor, about the organisation generally and about various matters related to their specific job responsibilities. Team briefing meetings should be short (say 20 minutes), informal and organised with some regularity. Nevertheless, the supervisor must prepare in advance, with a list of the matters to be covered. The meeting should provide opportunities for questions to be asked and answered and to review policy implementation, progress or successes, perceived difficulties etc. Team briefings could be used alternately with full staff meetings, but are more likely to be appropriate for the senior staff team or for small staff groups meeting in the middle of the day.

WRITTEN INFORMATION

Staff handbooks and noticeboards have an important role in the communication process, but they are limited by the fact that there is little opportunity for discussion about their contents between members of staff or with senior staff and the manager. Keeping written information up to date is the surest way of encouraging everyone to read, to take notice and to remember. This could be supplemented with an annual review exercise, perhaps asking for signatures to confirm that materials have been read by each member of staff. A checklist of all the official notices and practice guidelines to be displayed should also be maintained and the placement of notices should be monitored twice yearly.

INDIVIDUAL SUPERVISION

One to one sessions, between the manager and each member of staff, are used in a number of different situations. There are the interviews associated with probationary reviews, performance appraisal, disciplinary action and leaving employment.

There are also meetings to discuss specific things such as menu planning, projects to be undertaken, changes in staff duties, etc. which may require some planning and individual agreement on action to move things forward.

However, a regular programme of supervision sessions is different. Supervision meetings between the manager and each member of staff are used in many nurseries. There are some disadvantages to this method of staff management because it takes up a lot of managerial time and can be somewhat artificial if relationships are strained. Nevertheless, it has advantages in being a scheduled confidential opportunity for staff members to raise matters of concern and for the manager to advise them individually on performance. In general terms it encourages staff to take a professional approach to nursery work and contributes to the manager's knowledge of staff views.

Staff development and training

It is widely recognised that ongoing staff development and training programmes, provided by employers, are of significance in maintaining quality standards and achieving business success. In part, this is because the better trained the staff are, the better the service they will deliver. In a field like childcare, attendance at training courses, conferences, etc. helps to keep staff focused, challenged and up-to-date in their thinking, thus leading to a redefining and refining of nursery practice. The other way in which training impacts on the overall success of a service is that it leads managers to look more closely at how they organise and make use of the particular skills of staff, which in turn leads to a closer monitoring of all aspects of the organisation. The investment required to provide a good in-service training programme is not insubstantial but businesses of all sizes report that there is a return which makes it worthwhile, even in the short term.

SOURCES OF TRAINING

The definition of what constitutes training can be quite wide. A good nursery manager has a training function through acting as a role model and through all forms of interaction with the staff team. More experienced staff should have a similar training role with less experienced carers. A well-stocked staff room library and subscriptions to a range of suitable magazines are training resources. Places can be purchased on conferences and courses being offered by academic institutions, voluntary organisations or commercial establishments. Trainers can be commissioned to run courses for the whole staff group in the nursery. A good mix of types of training will be the most beneficial to your nursery and to individual staff members.

TRAINING NEEDS ANALYSIS

A regular analysis of all the skills and knowledge base amongst everyone involved in the nursery is recommended. So too is a study of the general levels of

Training Plan

Element one: individual skills

Type of training	Source	Result/application
	External sessions with:	
■ First Aid	■ Red Cross/St John's Ambulance	■ Full certificate
■ First Aid	■ Red Cross/St John's Ambulance	■ Updated certificate
■ NVQ Assessor	■ Local assessment centre	■ Assessor registration
■ NVQ assessment in: Childcare Catering	■ Local assessment centre	■ NVQ in: Childcare Catering
■ Safe food handling	■ Local environmental health	■ Certificate
■ Early years education in: National Curriculum Pre-maths Pre-reading Music Early science Technology	■ University	■ Attendance certificate

Element two: group skills development

Type of training	Source	Result/application
	In-house sessions with:	
■ Ensuring equal opportunities	■ CRE and independent trainers	■ Policy implementation
■ Anti-racism in practice	■ Early years anti-racist training network	■ Strategies for working with children
■ Local education policies	■ Local early years department	■ Policy and implementation
■ Curriculum development	■ Independent trainers	■ Strategies for working with children
■ Hygiene	■ Local environmental health	■ Procedures development
■ Health and Safety	■ HSE and independent trainers	■ Information/skills in risk assessment

Element three: personal development

These are examples only. The individual member of staff will take the lead in identifying training.

Type of training	Source	Result/application
	(In staff's own time)	
■ Early years education	■ Institute of Education	■ B.Ed. degree
■ Assertiveness	■ Voluntary sector courses	■ Personal growth
■ Women in management	■ Industrial society	■ Personal growth
■ Business management	■ Local enterprise centre ■ Local chamber of commerce	

Example of a training plan

competence in childcare and nursery management. Following this it is important to draw up, and maintain, a training plan for the nursery. This should have both short term and longer term goals and should include all the training needed to maintain your legal and registration obligations such as first aid and food handling. It should also include training which will support the nursery enrolment profile and enrich the programme, e.g. baby resuscitation techniques, pre-maths activities, Montessori practices, providing for special needs children, or swimming instruction and life-saving qualifications. Training needs identified by members of staff should be added. For example, staff might express an interest in the use of fire appliances, baby first aid, introduction to management, or report writing skills. The training plan should have some set priorities and targets for achievement. It will be necessary to decide which members of staff are to be offered particular types of training, whilst also allowing everyone a chance to indicate their personal preferences. Training should be equally on offer to everyone, based on equal opportunities and fair employment ethics.

TRAINING DAYS

There is something to be said for training staff together as a group. The training can be tailored to meet the nursery's priorities, may well cost less than a selection of other courses and should enhance the effectiveness of the team as a whole. However, it is more difficult to arrange as it has to be carried out when the nursery is closed and the issues of staff pay, time and family responsibilities impinge. Provided that it is built into the contract with parents and sufficient notice is given an annual training day can, of course, be held on a weekday. Otherwise it would need to take place on a weekend, and rely on the offer of a decent remuneration package and the general goodwill of all members of staff.

NATIONAL VOCATIONAL QUALIFICATIONS (NVQ)

If the nursery employs carers who do not have a recognised qualification, they could be offered opportunities to work towards an NVQ. There are several ways of doing this. You could set up your own assessment centre, but this involves complex and time-consuming work which may not be worthwhile for a small nursery. The nursery could join a local NVQ consortium or alternatively could buy in the services of the nearest assessment centre. In every circumstance, there will be registration fees to pay and charges for the services of an assessor to test the candidates on a unit by unit basis. Some NVQ candidates will need to have some formal training at a college in order to have the underpinning knowledge prerequisite to completing the units. Discussions with the local TEC and NVQ assessment centre will help identify the suitable options, the potential costs and any possible help with funding. The nursery manager should then be able to discuss with staff what training support can be offered.

Conclusion

The manager is key to the quality of the nursery and has to qualify as the Fit Person for registration purposes. Nevertheless, the competence and commitment of the whole staff team are highly important too. Training and development plans are significant for developing the skills of the team and for improving quality standards. A management structure which is underpinned by respect for staff members, and which values and involves them in planning, policy review and delegated responsibilities is the most suitable for a nursery.

Regulations governing the registration of the nursery are the foundations on which to base the staff profile and basic training plans. Advice on general management techniques is grounded in other business sectors, so publications from organisations such as the Industrial Society and the Institute for Personnel and Development are worth consulting.

CHECKLIST

- Staff profile with qualifications and experience
- Shift patterns to accommodate a range of expectations
- Arrangements to cover for planned staff absences
- Clarity in the manager's role and authority
- Structures to support the management style
- Team building
- Staff involvement
- Staff supervision
- Communications strategy
- Staff meetings
- Team briefing meetings
- Training needs analysis
- Training and development plan

8 MANAGING THE NURSERY

> **What this chapter covers:**
> - **The context**
> - **Policies and information**
> - **Enrolment profile and admission policies**
> - **Age groupings and social organisation**
> - **Equipment**
> - **Record keeping**
> - **The daily routine and rota of duties**

We are what we repeatedly do. Excellence then, is not an act, but a habit.

Aristotle

This chapter touches on the majority of those aspects which have to be managed as part of the start up and part of the ongoing process of providing good day care and education in a nursery. Providers may need to undertake further reading to gain an in-depth understanding of the full scope of the management issues.

Orchestrating the interplay of philosophy, legalities and practicalities is what day-to-day nursery management is about. There are diverse and competing demands in the form of staff management, policies, budgets, children's needs and parents expectations. Nursery management requires a fundamental understanding of general management issues balanced by a thorough understanding of the special nature and imperatives of professional childcare.

The context

The Children Act 1989 is the key piece of legislation which covers most legal matters relating to children. One section of it places duties and powers on local authorities to ensure minimum standards of care for young children. Volume 2 of the Guidance and Regulations attached to the Children Act sets out in detail the childcare-related standards which nurseries are expected to meet. The registration and annual inspection processes, which all nurseries must satisfy, arise from the duties placed on the local authorities. Alongside the Children Act, the legal context for nursery management also includes a diverse range of legislation and case law, including laws relating to employment, equal opportunities, health and safety, finance and accountancy. All nursery owners, managers and staff should be familiar with the Children Act Guidance and should be aware of the other areas of relevant legislation.

EXPECTED STANDARDS

One of the prerequisites for registration is a sensible management framework which focuses on good practice in childcare and education. Particular notice must be paid to the fact that the child's welfare is paramount and there is a duty of care for children attending the nursery. All nursery practice must ensure the safety of the children, generally meet their best interests, and operate in harmony with the requirements of all the relevant registration and inspection bodies. The nursery must also demonstrate due regard to the language, culture and religion of each child enrolled. Provision for children with special needs must take account of the Department for Education and Employment (DfEE) Code of Practice for Special Educational Needs.

A management framework which allows the nursery to be responsive to parents, children and staff as well as to adapt to changing demands in care and education will be the most successful in delivering a good service. Nevertheless, it will also need to support consistently the fundamental values and nursery programme which you purport to offer to children and families. Parents and others will expect to be assured that what the nursery proclaims it offers will be delivered.

PARENTAL FOCUS

Recognition of the significance of the parental role in the care and education of children is fundamental to the context in which nurseries operate. The Children Act offers guidance on parental roles and responsibilities. Parents have duties to protect their children and to promote their welfare. They are the child's first educators. They have special knowledge of their child's health, previous experiences and the family culture. Nursery practice needs to acknowledge this by respecting, consulting and involving parents as much as possible.

Policies and information

Establishing a comprehensive policy framework will go a long way to ensuring that the management of your nursery will flow coherently regardless of the ups and downs, overwork and mini crises which will undoubtedly occur over time. There are many practical uses for written policies such as in staff induction, for informing parents, and for monitoring quality standards. Some will be required as part of the local authority registration process whilst others will emerge, e.g. from the way the nursery space is organised, the type of programme being offered and the ages of children enrolled. Policies are the cornerstones of nursery management.

FRAMING POLICY

Policy writing takes some thought. Policies have to encompass your beliefs and values as well as making clear what action will be pursued and how. However, they should be succinct and easily understood to facilitate implementation. Sometimes managers and others look on policy writing as an 'organisational nicety', but that is a naive perception. Without written policies you cannot hope to maintain a shared understanding of how the nursery operates, with coherent and consistent performance from the nursery staff, and confident cooperation from parents.

Some managers regard 'buying in' commercially prepared policies as a practical solution, an instant route to success. However, this is nearly as useless as having no policies at all. Without policies being written to reflect the real values, quality standards and unique character of your nursery, you will be faced with uncertainties over what interpretation is intended. Through writing the policies yourself (and hopefully including the staff group too) you will be able to tease out unexpected questions and grey areas of management for which you will need to make provision. Policies are the baselines that underpin every decision that is taken every day by everyone involved with the nursery. They are a reference point for staff, parents and inspection bodies.

COMMUNICATIONS

Policies need to be shared and communicated. Information acquisition and exchange are central to the formation and application of policies. Managers need information about issues and values in order to first frame, then monitor, policies. Child care staff need to know about policies in order to inform their way of working. Parents need to know in order to make enrolment choices and set their expectations. Unless information is exchanged and policies are communicated, there can be no clear monitoring of quality or identification of gaps in practice.

Communication within the staff team
There are a number of communication strategies including induction training, staff meetings, handbooks, verbal presentations, information leaflets and posters. General staff meetings provide opportunities for full discussion of the implications of policies and the development of strategies for successfully implementing them. Regular reviews of policies by the manager and the staff group should lead to useful additions or revisions which enhance practice and expand the extent to which principles are commonly held.

Communication with parents
Parents should be within the nursery's policy and information loop. For example, they need to know about general policies, quality standards, learning objectives, qualifications of staff and the philosophy which underpins the service. They should also be informed about what will happen if there is an accident or their child takes sick at nursery and circumstances under which it might be necessary to exclude their child. An information leaflet which provides sufficient detail and explains your intentions, as well as some of the regulatory framework within which the nursery operates, will help to meet the nursery's obligations to parents. Supplementary information through the use of posters, notices, parents'

evenings and individual discussions are also essential. Parents who find it difficult to understand information in English should be given special consideration
and translations if possible. Conscientious sharing of information in a number of
different ways, should prevent misunderstandings and also help parents to fulfil
their roles and responsibilities in relation to nursery services. Parents have a
right to know what to expect, including information about relatively sensitive
policy issues such as health promotion, equality and child protection. This is
where knowing what you mean and meaning what you say has particular importance!

Enrolment profile and admission policies

The nursery enrolment profile – the ages and numbers of children – will largely
be dictated by what the layout of the nursery premises allows in terms of clear
space and size of rooms. The enrolment profile links directly to the business
plan, because of the requirements for equipment, numbers of staff and their
qualifications. So the profile should be carefully modelled and adjusted as necessary until it provides the best possible plan. The profile has to match up to a
combination of meeting local needs, use of space and realistic budgets, whilst still
complying with registration requirements. The profile may have to be revised
over time as needs change. Key areas to watch include numbers of new children
to admit en bloc or as phased admissions, part-time places and settling in times.

FAIR PLAY

Equal opportunity issues should have a high profile in practices of enrolling children. Admission criteria, the management of waiting lists and nursery publicity
should not favour any one group of people. It can be fair to give admission priority to children taking up full-time places, provided that this is made clear in
publicity etc. It is not fair to keep names on a waiting list without providing
information about how the waiting list operates and without managing the list on
anything other than a first come basis.

BALANCED ADMISSIONS

It may be tempting for financial reasons to enrol as many children as possible
regardless of their ages and the number of sessions they wish to attend. But you
should be aware of the importance of having a balanced intake. You cannot provide a good standard of care if , for example, you have more babies than you can
settle in happily or if you have limitations on sleeping arrangements or nappy
changing facilities. You cannot expect to have a smooth flow of enrolments if a
large group of the children are likely to leave en bloc when they reach school
age. You cannot demonstrate a commitment to children's best interests if you
enrol children for only a few hours per week – they will not have enough time at
nursery to make sense of it.

WAITING LIST RECORD SHEET

Child's name _____

Parents' names _____

Home address _____

_____

Contact telephone numbers _____

_____

Child's d.o.b. _____

Preferred start date _____

Alternatives _____

Week days needed _____

Alternatives _____

Last possible date for decision _____

_____

Literature checklist	
Item	Date
Prospectus	
Waiting list policy	
Contract and fees	

Review of status on waiting list

Date for first review _____

Date parents contacted _____

Notes from first review discussion with parents _____

_____

Date for next review _____

Date parents contacted _____

Notes _____

_____

Final review _____

_____

Date parents contacted _____

Example of a waiting list record sheet

Age groupings and social organisation

There are undoubtedly fashions in thinking about how to group children during the nursery day. However, it does seem to be particularly practical to group them by age. In fact, the registration regulations set by some local authorities require the separation of the under-twos. Nevertheless, there is considerable benefit to all the children, and especially to siblings, if older and younger children can spend some part of the day together. All children learn from each other and gain additional social skills, confidence and independence through building relationships with children of other ages. Flexibility in grouping allows opportunities for younger children to play in more sophisticated ways with more complex equipment. They can test out their skills and learn from older children. Mixed groupings allow older children time to recognise their own strengths and to develop finer understandings of the other children's vulnerabilities.

To facilitate some shared time, the staff will need to make some fine judgments about the safety and learning issues as well as about how to organise variations in parts of the day. Staff will need to plan carefully and develop a range of programmes as well as having an agreed protocol for who can decide about individual children moving between age groups.

INDIVIDUAL DIFFERENCES

Flexibility to allow children to interact with other children of their own choice and to find their own level of activity is good practice. After all, each child is an individual. Some children will be more socially mature than their age suggests. Some will be stronger in one skill than another. Some will need more emotional security at one time than at another. Of course, adult support and organisation will be necessary. Adults must remember to take their lead from the children rather than simply prejudge what might seem appropriate from the adult perspective.

Parents should be informed about how and why the children are grouped. Some sensitivity is needed to ensure that parents do not think that their child is being left behind whilst another is 'promoted' to an older group.

Equipment

It is staggering just what a wide variety and quantity of equipment is needed in a nursery. It goes without saying that your expenditure on equipment will be a significant part of the budget and consequently value for money will be an issue. However, you should be sure that you focus on value rather than on price. As tempting as it might be to purchase items second hand, you should be very cautious about doing so. The safety aspects are so important in childcare that taking a risk is foolish. Also there are issues about the aesthetics of stocking a nursery with used items. To create a positive ambience and visual environment all items, decor and storage furniture should be harmonious. Children are sensitive to their surroundings.

Unpacking and assembling equipment is a serious activity

SELECTION CRITERIA

Nursery equipment should be selected by three criteria: suitability, versatility and durability.

To be suitable, equipment has to fit in with the type of programme you plan and be appropriate for the ages of the children, as well as being safe, and in harmony with the scale and design of the nursery premises. It also has to be free from any hidden negative messages related to gender, ability or race, etc. and to reflect positively the plurality of society.

Selecting for versatility includes consideration of how many ways an item can be used, whether indoors or out, by one child or a group and whether it is sufficiently open-ended in use to allow children to direct their own play.

Durability encompasses safety and hygiene features, cleaning possibilities, maintenance and repair options as well as general robustness.

Building up a very broad-based collection of equipment over time is a good idea. For example, children's individual interests, seasonal projects and cultural festivals all need particular equipment – especially items which are unlikely to be found in commercial toy suppliers.

COMPUTERS

Information technology (computers and CD ROMs etc.) is growing in significance for nursery programmes and deserves separate consideration. Choices of software should be made with a view to offering opportunities to children at various developmental stages and with a range of abilities and interests – to include children who can make use of the technology without adult supervision.

Programmes need to be varied in focus and to offer a progressive understanding of technology. The selection of software programmes should support creativity and imagination as well as numeracy and literacy. Software should have some form of built-in feedback or reward for the children who use it. How beneficially the equipment is used will depend on the technological confidence of the staff and the support they can give to the children to use it. Consequently, staff training should be treated as part of the equipment package!

INITIAL EQUIPMENT FOR THE NEW NURSERY

If your nursery is in the start-up phase it is worthwhile making extensive, detailed lists of all the equipment you think you will need, or want, to support your planned programme. The list can be developed by sitting down with a selection of catalogues and an experienced nursery worker. It can be augmented by visiting one or two established nurseries where you can see what is popular and how children and staff are using the equipment.

Whilst you will not have to buy everything before you open, you will need to have the basics and enough equipment to provide a very wide variety of activities for the children. Just because only a few children are enrolled is not sufficient reason to have only a few pieces of play equipment. Those children will need the full range of experiences and will not want to repeat the same activities too frequently.

SUFFICIENT SUPPLIES

Do not forget that duplication of many items may be necessary as a way of offering an appropriate programme for the children (so that more than one group of children can be playing in a home corner or having tea at the same time) and making the best use of staff time (so that they are with the children, not searching around for a particular item). Some examples of duplicates likely to be needed are water/sand trays, painting easels, sterilisers, food serving trolleys, sheets, blankets and dust pans and brushes. You will also have to plan to have a sufficient supply of items such as puzzles, Lego pieces, scissors, building blocks, cot sheets, children's mugs, children's chairs, storage boxes and baskets. Some labour saving equipment will help too, e.g. electric bottle warmers and hand-held vacuum cleaners.

DELIVERY OF NEW EQUIPMENT

Unpacking, assembling and arranging new equipment is a serious and time-consuming activity. At start-up it can take three or four days. This is a process which should not just be left to chance. You may require some additional labour and particular tools to assemble heavy furniture etc. It is definitely something which at least the core staff should be involved in – so that they know what equipment there is, where it is stored, how things work, where instructions are filed, etc. Some of the tasks involved are:

■ unpacking and checking the condition of items delivered

- matching items delivered against the delivery note and the order form
- assembling flat packed items such as cots, bookcases, tables etc.
- safety checking to make sure there is nothing loose, no rough edges, no hygiene worries etc.
- planning the location of items for staff efficiency, safety and protection for children
- organising storage for domestic items, cot sheets, bulk supplies, etc.
- locking away cleaning supplies and other toxic or dangerous substances
- organising suitable storage containers for small items of play equipment
- labelling items so children can identify them and storing items so children can have access to them
- washing and putting away cooking utensils, cutlery, etc.
- stocking the refrigerator and freezer and setting the temperatures correctly.

Record keeping

Keeping records is an essential part of managing a nursery. Some records must be kept as a matter of legal obligation, others are necessary to facilitate running the business, while even more are part and parcel of good practice in childcare and education. Confidentiality is a major issue when you hold so much personal information. You will need to be sure that everyone in the nursery is committed to maintaining confidentially and to have a secure place to keep the most sensitive records.

If you keep good records you can be sure that you are prepared to meet any enquiries about a child's welfare or any legalistic eventuality, and you will have sufficient management information to review important aspects of your nursery business. Good records will also allow you to monitor your quality standards with some confidence. You should expect to retain your records for several years. A period of six years is required for tax purposes, and it is a good rule of thumb for all other records as well.

CHILDCARE RECORDS

Those records which have basic information about the children enrolled are key to the day-to-day management of the nursery. Generally they have a format which is fairly standard amongst nurseries and conforms to registration requirements. Your local authority registration officer can advise you on this. The main records are listed below and the list is annotated to include some reminders about information which is too often overlooked, but which is highly useful to collect:

- child record – be sure to include dietary information, health and immunisation details, home language and religion, any custody arrangements and alternative contacts for emergencies
- baby and toddler enrolment questionnaire – be sure to include sleeping patterns, breast or bottle feeding times, introduction of solids, food preferences, toilet training plan, fears and main causes of tears

- daily attendance register – be sure to include contact numbers for parents, monitoring of reasons for absence
- administration of medicines form – be sure to include parental permission and instructions, double signatures confirming each dose given
- accident book and reports – be sure to include treatment given, names of witnesses, time of leaving the nursery
- suspected child abuse forms – be sure to include large diagrams on which any marks can be noted, dates of confidences or observations, parents' comments, names of professionals contacted about concerns and dates of contact
- child assessment records – be sure to include names of friends, milestones, significant achievements related to curriculum goals, parents' comments/ contributions
- permissions forms for outings or other events – be sure to include details of the purpose of the event, safety precautions to be taken, options for parents to choose not to give permission and their reasons.

GENERAL RECORDS

A daily diary and a day book are very useful records to keep up to date. They should include details of which staff were present in the nursery and when, any visitors and prospective parents, conferences with individual parents, unusual occurrences, problems with the services, e.g. power cuts or gas leaks, and details of children's outings, etc. They can serve as an *aide-mémoire* if you need to reflect on a series of events and can help to substantiate details if there is a complaint, accident investigation, legal action or enquiry of a similar nature.

MENUS

Written menus should be produced, and retained on file, so that there is a record of what food, including alternatives, has been served each day. The usual purposes of the written menus are for planning the purchase of food and to inform parents of what has been provided for their child. However, it is important to keep the menus as a record which can be used to reflect back on nutritional standards generally. It is also important that there is some record in case children become ill as a result of what they have eaten or are subsequently diagnosed as having allergies.

LEARNING PROGRAMME PLANNING RECORDS

The planning matrix, project web, or whatever mechanisms you use for recording your plans for learning activities, should be filed together with any supporting documentation and photographs. Not only will they serve as a way of monitoring and reviewing your curriculum or inspiring new work, but also they will be essential tools to use in meetings with new staff members, parents, inspection officers and other professional visitors.

BUSINESS RECORDS

All the records related to finance and personnel matters such as: the business accounts, invoices raised, budgets and expenditure against budget, petty cash, bank reconciliation, payroll, SSP and PAYE, individual employee's details, staff sickness absences, staff holidays, etc. are required to support your legal obligations and your business needs. Health and safety records fall into a similar category. A number of forms for the record systems are provided by the relevant statutory agencies, and commercial companies also supply useful documentation. Your accountant and bank manager are likely to stipulate what records they want you to keep and to offer advice on formats which will produce the information which they particularly need.

The daily routine and rota of staff duties

Fitting everything into the nursery day takes some careful planning. It also requires a level of efficiency and sensitivity from the staff who have to be able to work generally to a schedule, whilst maintaining a relaxed atmosphere, and without placing too many restrictions on the children's choices and pursuits.

The routine is best written on a single page, showing time slots against events in the day (see the example on the next page). Staff need to know what general time frame is planned for each part of the day.

The rota of staff duties should be outlined on one sheet, so that staff can see at a glance what they are meant to be doing. More detailed listing of rota duties, matched to the needs of the daily routine (e.g. setting up for lunch), may also be needed.

The routine and rota are best kept under constant review and adjusted whenever necessary in order to provide the richest possible experiences for the children.

THE ROUTINE FOR BABIES

There generally needs to be a separate routine for babies. This is because babies are best served if their own natural, individual routines are followed. It means turning the usual understanding of a nursery routine on its head by having an absolute minimum of fixed points in the day – the arrivals and departures of the babies.

THE ROUTINE FOR OLDER CHILDREN

For the older children (toddlers upwards) the routine should have allocated times for meals, rest, free play, structured activities, outdoor activities, quiet activities and special activities. It needs to be planned to accommodate the period of time during which children will be arriving and leaving the nursery, when activities must be organised on a telescoping basis. It needs to allow time for the

A nursery routine

The daily routine of the nursery is not rigid, but it is important to provide a structure which the children and staff can follow.

8.00 a.m.	**Welcome**	Nursery set up ready for children. Breakfast available. Toast, cereal, etc.
9.00 a.m.	**Free play**	Wide range of activities suited to age and children's needs, all supervised by an adult to encourage language, confidence and independence. Art activities, malleable, construction, puzzles etc.
10.30 a.m.	**Break/snack time**	Stop activity time. A time for children to be calm, listen and join in with games, songs, music, drama. Refreshments available, milk, juice, fruit, raisins, biscuits.
11.00 a.m.	**Garden open**	An opportunity to let off steam, run around, develop gross motor skills; adult supervised. Activities in nursery still available for stimulation and more adult interaction.
12.00 p.m.	**Lunchtime**	Family style, children involved in helping set tables, serve, clear away.
12.45 p.m.	**Bathroom**	Encouraging personal care, toilet, wash, brush hair, clean teeth.
1.00 p.m.	**Rest time**	Sleep for younger children and a rest for older ones if necessary.
2.00 p.m.	**Free play**	Short outings may take place to local shops, swimming, parks, farms.
3.00 p.m.	**Breaktime**	Refreshments available, music, drama, group activities.
3.30 p.m.	**Garden**	Adult supervised, as in morning.
4.00 p.m.	**Tea time**	Family style, as lunch.
4.30 p.m.	**Relaxation**	Calm environment, group activities, lotto, table toys, stories, books.
6.15 p.m.	**Goodbye**	Staff clear and tidy nursery.

Example of a daily routine

children's toileting and personal hygiene before meals. It should provide opportunities for a choice of activities to be taking place simultaneously and the flexibility to allow for such things as making use of outdoor space in good weather. It has to take account of staff shift patterns in order to provide continuity for the most focused activities. And, of course, it has to fit with the practicalities facing the cook in preparing meals on time.

ACCOMMODATING INDIVIDUALS

Whilst it is not suggested that 'special areas' or 'school rooms' should be set up, it is suggested that opportunities for additional challenges for some children in the nursery should be built into the routine. These have to be planned on the basis of children's individual circumstances. For example, some children need less rest and more stimulation during the day than others. Some children need a particular type of preparation for school. One child may be gifted and another may have a disability. Whatever the children's needs are, the additional challenge programme must not be a burden to them. Particular care should be taken to plan and manage the daily routine in a way which ensures that the children who do need special challenges do not miss out on the mainstream activities with their peers.

STAFF ROTAS

Successfully maintaining the routine each day depends largely on the staff rota of duties. Every member of staff should know what is expected of them in relation to each part of the nursery routine. Who sets up the equipment and activities in the morning? Who makes up the babies' bottles and sterilises them during the day? Who organises breakfast and clears away? Who cleans the tables in preparation for lunch and cleans up and mops the floor afterwards? Who monitors the condition of the toilet area and disinfects it as needed during the day? Who sets out the rest mattresses, sorts out the linen, etc.? Who comforts the children and stays with them as they go to sleep? Who organises the morning and afternoon snacks? Who takes which activities during the day? Who supervises the outside play space? Who covers for non-contact time in order for staff to make observations and maintain assessment records? Who covers for who during lunch breaks or whilst some staff are out of the nursery through taking a group of children on an outing? And so on.

The rota should be organised in a way which is both practical and fair to everyone. No member of staff wants to always have to wash the paint pots on a Friday, or clear up from lunch each day. Clearly the shift patterns have an influence on who does what on the rota and consequently it can be sensible to link rota duties to shifts. Sometimes, the rota has to be linked to staff working in a particular area of the nursery. However, using a combination of ways to work out the rota offers a useful flexibility which may best support the daily routine.

Conclusion

The diversity of tasks involved in the day-to-day nursery management is wide and almost unlimited. To a large extent, management is about recognising and addressing all the sub-tasks which constitute every area of work, and linking these to the wider issues. Nursery management goes hand in hand with the building of the staff team and the development of the skills of each staff member.

Sources of advice and information are extensive. However, the starting point should be the local authority Registration Guidance, and the Children Act Guidance Volume 2. Voluntary organisations, such as the National Early Years Network, sell a range of very useful guides. Play equipment suppliers produce extensive catalogues, some of which are well organised and designed to support clear understandings of the issues involved in choosing and using equipment.

CHECKLIST

Legal context
- Children Act
- Registration and inspection
- Duty of care for children
- Health and safety
- Employment

Management framework
- Policies and practice guidelines
- Quality standards
- Information for parents
- Staff communications
- Rota of duties
- Record keeping

Provision for children
- Enrolment profile
- Grouping children
- Flexibility and individual needs
- Daily routine
- Plans for learning activities
- Equipment selection and maintenance

9 THE CHILDCARE PROGRAMME

> **What this chapter covers:**
> - Age differences
> - An appropriate ethos
> - Settling in children
> - Managing children's behaviour
> - Child protection
> - Child health
> - Diet, nutrition and mealtimes

One never notices what has been done; one can only see what remains to be done.

Marie Curie

This chapter focuses on care, which nurseries are expected to provide. It relates specifically to those aspects of the nursery programme which are not linked to learning. Care is sometimes deemed to be a sort of secondary consideration. Nevertheless, the issues are numerous and they impinge significantly on quality. They are also generally more complex than may be realized; inevitably providers will find it necessary to undertake additional reading but the main issues are outlined below.

In order to achieve good outcomes for children a nursery has to succeed at a number of tasks. These include maintaining the right balance between what is appropriate for each individual child and what suits the general age and stage of development of children generally within their peer group. The nursery must also adopt a comprehensive approach to the provision of both education and care, which have a mutually significant role in children's growth and development. The primary focus of the care element is the children's physical, emotional and social development.

Age differences

Young children's needs wax and wane at various ages and stages of their development. However, whatever their age, they require nurturing, protection and sensitive responses from all the adults with whom they have contact.

BABIES

Babies, under one year old, are very vulnerable. Continuity of carers is significant because of the need to responsibly monitor each baby's health and comfort, and because of the crucial importance of the emotional attachments which help a baby to feel safe and happy. Babies usually have their own natural routine, which it is best to follow, even in the nursery. On average, they can be expected to sleep about 60 per cent of the day although individual babies obviously vary considerably. The remainder of their day is mostly taken up with feeding and nappy changing. However, such necessities also present rich opportunities for those all important cuddles and close communications. Most babies in a nursery are likely to be used to a combination of both breast and bottle feeding and first foods. No baby should ever be just left with a bottle, to feed alone. This is dangerous and emotionally destructive. As babies' eyes, bowels and muscles develop they gain a degree of control over their bodies. With the strength to stretch, roll, sit, crawl and stand they begin to take a greater interest in their environment. So, from the time they are able to sit up, babies will be happier if they are propped up in a safe place to observe what is going on around them and to facilitate their interaction with the adults caring for them.

EARLY TODDLERS

Early toddlers are more robust than babies, but still need a lot of care and protection. They are often clingy with their parents and main carers. They are likely to be easily upset by changes in routine and need lots of cuddles and continuity. Early toddlers may still want to be picked up and carried a lot, even though they will be excitedly enjoying their newly developed walking abilities. They will also be maturing in a number of other ways. They will begin to try to use language to communicate. Increased hand and eye co-ordination will allow them to enjoy a wider range of simple toys. They will be interested in trying to feed themselves. Toilet training may begin when their physical development allows. Although they will probably need to have two naps daily, children at the early toddler stage will be alert and active for most of the day. Acknowledgment of other children will lay the foundations of future close friendships.

OLDER TODDLERS

Older toddlers can be fairly independent, but they need considerable sensitive support and positive adult interaction to help them cope with the range of emotions which they are beginning to develop. Insecurity, frustration and fear will be their predominant emotions for much of the time as they become more aware of the world and try to master their new-found skills and physical development. Older toddlers will be able to run, jump, go up and down stairs and partially dress or undress themselves. Tooth care should become an important part of their personal hygiene regime. They will probably be potty trained and dry during the day, although there may be periods of regression. Children at this stage will usually need only one long nap during the day. Friendly interactions with other children will take up a significant part of their time, but frustration with some activities and lack of understanding of the concepts of sharing or taking turns may make playing together difficult.

OVER THREES

Three to five year old children are able to be quite independent. However, when they are hurt, worried or frightened, they need sympathetic comforting and sensible explanations. They are likely to respond best to ritual, routine and the familiar, as important emotional props. At this stage children will have good physical co-ordination and control so that they can jump, climb nimbly, and stand on one foot. They will be able to care for themselves to a large extent, e.g. going to the toilet by themselves, washing their own hands and brushing their teeth. Children of this age may or may not need a nap during the day, but they will certainly benefit from having a period of quiet in the middle of the day. They will engage in co-operative activities with other children and are likely to be emotionally mature enough to negotiate over most conflicts.

An appropriate ethos

Quality of life is undoubtedly important. For children attending a nursery this is largely dependent on the ethos within which the nursery operates and how that is supported by the management structure. A positive recognition of how children's needs differ is part and parcel of the ethos. For example, the routine for babies needs to emulate their individual natural patterns. This is completely different to the group-based routine needed by four year olds.

The nursery must be a happy and stress-free place which promotes self-esteem in each child and helps to build their self-confidence. Put in very basic terms, this means that there should be laughter and genuine expressions of affection and friendship. Adults should act as good role models; children should treat each other with respect and kindness; children should be offered a variety of opportunities to express themselves; no adult voices should be raised and no child should be shamed or mocked or made to feel badly about themselves!

The nursery's attitude to parents is an equally significant part of the ethos. It is important to recognise that parents are the child's primary carers and that the parent–nursery relationship should be one of shared care. Responding to expressed parental preferences for the child, consulting parents and mutually agreeing plans related to the child's health and development, as well as sharing information and resources, are vital to building an ethos beneficial to the children.

SELF-ESTEEM AND INDIVIDUALITY

Having regard for children's self-esteem is an integral part of the caring ethos. This includes treating each child and their parents with respect and courtesy, as well as encouraging all the children to be kind to each other. Finding ways to praise children for their achievements and displaying their work are important. So too are creating opportunities for all children to have a role in 'helping' in the nursery (e.g. setting the table for lunch) and 'participating' in larger nursery activities (e.g. singing as part of a party entertainment). Particular effort should be made to offer equally valuable opportunities to children with special needs or disabilities and to provide them with positive images. Similarly, positive reflection of the languages, religions and cultural identities of all the children and their families not only helps to enrich general knowledge, but also demonstrates the nursery's commitment to an inclusive and holistic approach. This positive commitment should encompass the choice of displays, posters, music tapes, reading books, daily menus, celebrations, pretend food in the home corner and dressing up clothes, etc.

Children need to have their individuality recognised and to be treated as special individuals. In terms of activities, the availability of a range of options and opportunities to make choices supports individuality. So too do things such as conversations at circle time, photographs of nursery events, themes and displays based on family trees, celebrations of birthdays and acknowledgment of new siblings. Knowing that name-signs or photographs are used to designate their individual place to hang outdoor clothes, that a special place is designated to keep each child's own special creams and spare indoor clothes, and that a particular place is designated for storing drawings and other work, reinforces a child's feeling of belonging to the group whilst also being regarded as 'special'.

How to support children's individuality

- **Preparations for starting at nursery**
  Parents advised what personal items to bring
  Labelled coat peg
  Labelled container for clothes, etc.
  Labelled folder or drawer for collection of 'work'
  Birthday marked in nursery diary
  Keyworker on hand to say welcome

- **Ongoing arrangements**
  Keyworker maintains contact
  Known by name by other children
  Particular special interests are known by all
  Labelled chair
  Personalised place mat or similar
  Name on birthday chart
  Photograph in nursery photo album

- **Chosen regularly to participate or take the lead**
  Sharing news or a point of view
  Acting as a lunch time helper
  Choosing a story or song for circle time
  Telling a story
  Joining a member of staff on a trip to the local shop
  Visiting the library
  Starring in a birthday celebration tea
  Making a family tree

Example of a checklist: some ways of supporting individual identity

CONFIDENCE

A commitment to building self-confidence is a significant part of the ethos. Really there are two aspects to this. First there is the matter of helping each child to feel comfortable in the nursery setting. Secondly there is the need to develop self-confidence. Confidence is a prerequisite base for children to be able to strive to reach their full potential, especially in terms of their intellectual development. There are a number of methods which seem to work well for building confidence.

A key worker system ensures that each child has at least one special adult to relate to, who understands and encourages them and who can especially provide care and comfort at times of ill health or emotional upset. Being a part of a small group of children and adults builds friendships and a significant support network offering consistency and affection. Having a regular routine in the nursery endows each day with a comforting familiarity. The company of a sympathetic adult whilst drifting off to sleep at rest time and (perhaps grumpily) waking up again is a high priority in terms of comfort! Parental involvement in nursery activities, particularly during settling in and at the beginning or end of each day, makes sense of the significant links between home and nursery and between parents and nursery staff.

PHYSICAL DEVELOPMENT

Fostering children's physical development deserves attention as an important aspect of nursery life. This includes supporting both health and physical needs. Helping children to cope with their changing bodies and emerging skills takes patience and skill, usually best provided by the key workers and special adults who are most trusted and best known by the children. Adults have a key role in providing children with positive reinforcement, encouragement and examples of how to do things.

The daily routine should help children to develop good habits and ultimately to look after themselves by dressing, hand washing, tooth brushing, etc. Play and learning activities have to be structured to provide opportunities for the development of both large motor and fine co-ordination skills. Examples of large motor skills include: crawling, walking, running, climbing, balancing, cycling, throwing balls, digging in the garden and completing obstacle courses. Fine co-ordination skills include: grasping small toys, posting shapes, threading beads, sewing with yarn, painting with a brush, cutting with scissors and holding a pencil.

The layout of the nursery can facilitate the children's development. As babies they need safe areas in which to stretch out and then crawl; older children need large indoor and outdoor spaces to play in a physically challenging manner. As with other aspects of the care of children, close liaison between home and nursery is in the best interests of the children.

Settling in children

At the time of organising the enrolment, parents should be encouraged to consider how best to make the transition to nursery as easy as possible for their child. Settling-in is an important part of childcare and is particularly significant in a shared care partnership with parents. Time spent by the nursery manager and the parent going through all the child record forms and discussing the child's home routine, likes and dislikes, etc. is a worthwhile investment in preparing for a positive relationship. Similarly, a pre-enrolment visit to the nursery by the child and parent or a visit to the child's home by a member of the nursery staff can be a good starting point.

The length of time required for settling in, of course, will be different for each child and family and so a plan should be agreed between parent and nursery. A two- or three-stage process seems to work best. Arrangements should be made for parent and child to stay in the nursery together during the first day or two. This allows the child to share the nursery experience with their parent. It also allows the child time to build up friendships with other adults and children, and to become familiar with the surroundings and daily routine. After the initial few days the child should be left on their own in the nursery for short periods of time, which are gradually increased over a few days. This helps the child to acclimatise further and to build up confidence.

From the child's perspective, starting at nursery is, after all, quite a major life change! Nursery staff and parents must acknowledge the child's feelings about being left. Close contact with their key worker, and holding their favourite toy from home or a comfort blanket will help support the child emotionally. A cheery daily welcome, a cuddle and an invitation to join an activity will help a child to settle better at the beginning of each day.

Settling in times are important for parents as well as children. Parents need to feel confident that their child will be happy, stimulated and well cared for. This is especially significant for parents who may be having to cope with feelings of guilt or disappointment at having to leave their child. When planning your settling in process, you should consider ways of making parents feel comfortable in the nursery, e.g. by explaining the routine and asking them to assist the children in some simple tasks or activities. There also need to be opportunities for parents and key workers to get to know each other. As a follow-on, when children begin to attend the nursery without a parent being present, you might offer an open invitation for parents to telephone during the day, to put their minds at rest.

Managing children's behaviour

Understanding the child's point of view is a prerequisite for all adult interventions in their behaviour. Children experience the full spectrum of emotions including loneliness, hurt, insecurity, jealousy, grief, fear, anger, frustration and boredom. Such feelings must be respected and acknowledged. Often children have to cope with major life events such as the birth of a new baby, parental discord or divorce, or moving from one home to another. Sometimes they have acquired 'bad habits' through having poor role models to emulate. Sometimes they have adopted overly compliant behaviour in an effort to attract adult praise. In other instances they may have become withdrawn, depressed or developmentally regressed.

The adults involved in caring for children need good observational skills and knowledge of child development in order to understand each child's individual behaviour. Adults also must have good listening skills to foster regular one-to-one conversations and close supportive relationships with children. Knowing they are liked and respected by at least one special adult helps children to take up opportunities to confide their worries and feelings. With positive adult attention, help and guidance, children can usually come to terms with their emotions and develop appropriate behaviour patterns.

EXPECTATIONS

Nurseries have to have clear expectations of how children will interact with each other and with the adults. Adults must behave in keeping with the expectations so that they act as good role models. Children do need to have some limits set for them. The rules should be simple to understand as well as regularly enforced in a fair manner. The focus should include safety, consideration and respect for other people's feelings, the development of negotiation and sharing skills, and the building of friendships. No child should be slapped or frightened or humiliated. Adults must ensure that they criticise poor behaviour but do not criticise the child as a person. After all, no child is intrinsically bad or naughty. Being supportive, reinforcing good behaviour and redirecting behaviour into positive actions are the best strategies. Adults should also be able to anticipate when children may be at a sensitive stage, coming under pressure, likely to be provoked, or bored with the nursery activities. It is an adult responsibility to plan suitably, in advance, for the benefit of those children. The organisation of the nursery day and the management of the children's behaviour needs to take all factors into account.

It is clear that home and nursery expectations have to be co-ordinated as much as possible and nursery staff and parents must regularly discuss any concerns about the children. It is not just the parents of children who behave inappropriately who need to talk, but also the parents of children who may have been adversely affected by another child's actions. Without violating confidences, nursery staff do owe parents, and children, an explanation of developmental or behaviour difficulties. The shared care ethos and the nursery's policy on behaviour management should be set out in the documents providing information for parents. Instances of unmanageable behaviour, when outside professional interventions or exclusions from nursery may be necessary, should also be clarified in printed information to parents.

Nursery staff and parents must regularly discuss any concerns about the children

Child protection

As part of the registration process it will be necessary to develop a child protection policy for the nursery. If at all possible this should take account of procedures recommended by the local authority child protection committee. It is important that once developed, the policy is widely communicated and regularly reviewed. Every parent and member of staff needs to understand that child protection comes under the 'duty of care' for children attending the nursery. It should encompass both abuse and more general safety.

ABUSE

The definition of abuse is necessarily broad to include neglect and emotional abuse as well as physical and sexual abuse. Nursery staff may need training in how to identify abuse. It is likely that they may be the first to notice the signs or to be trusted with confidences by the children. Whenever abuse is identified, it must be faced up to. Any signs or suggestions of abuse, of whatever origin, must be noted and action taken in line with the advice of the statutory authorities. However, everyone involved will need a lot of support.

In addition to being expected to take action if abuse is recognised, all staff must be thoroughly vetted on appointment. As well as this, the nursery manager needs to organise close supervision for any students, temporary staff, probationary staff and nursery visitors (including parents and siblings) entering the nursery premises. Only adults who are qualified, established and vetted members of staff should be left alone in charge of children.

SAFETY

Nurseries have a duty to ensure that children are not put at risk during the nursery day. Every risk has to be anticipated.

Any documents which contain children's names together with their home addresses or other such information must be treated as highly confidential. They should not be left lying around, even in the nursery. It is crucial that only those who 'need to know' have access to details about children and families.

Arrival and departure

Arrangements for children arriving at the nursery in the morning and being collected at the end of the day must be tightly managed in order to prevent children wandering off on their own or being removed by someone who should not have access. Parents must be expected to accompany their child personally into the nursery in the morning and to ensure that a member of staff has taken charge of the child before they leave.

The nursery has to know if one parent is denied access by the courts, in order to prevent that parent from, improperly, removing the child from the nursery.

Only an adult (over 18 years old), who has been specifically named by a child's parent, and identified by the nursery staff, should be allowed to collect the child, when the parent is unable to do so.

Outings

Outings have to be planned and conducted in a manner which takes account of all the possible child protection issues. Precautions must be taken to eliminate any possibility of children wandering away from the group or being accosted, mistreated or abducted. For example, it is not a good idea to fix name badges obviously to children. An unknown person who can call a child by name may not be identified as a stranger by the child!

Child health

Good health has a major life-enhancing impact. Nurseries have a high level of responsibility for maintaining the good physical and emotional health of children. In fact, there is a two-fold responsibility; first for directly caring for and protecting the children enrolled in the nursery, and second for introducing the children to healthy lifestyles and helping them to learn to care for their own health and hygiene.

BABIES

Particular attention must be paid to caring for babies. The approach must be different to that for other age groups. Babies in group care must be enabled to follow their own natural rhythms and routines. Baby care requires a very thorough and experienced knowledge of the health and developmental issues involved. It is not just about changing nappies and giving bottles. It is about intelligent understanding and responsiveness, e.g. to:

- the significance of body temperature and dehydration
- the patterns of bowel and bladder functions
- the treatment of various forms of skin sensitivity
- the difficulties of teething
- the necessity to monitor sleeping babies
- the meanings of particular types and patterns of crying.

GROWING UP

As children grow and develop their ability to communicate with adults changes. They can give clearer indications about when they are thirsty, how they are feeling or what hurts. However, their vulnerabilities change too. For example, they begin to encounter a wider range of possible triggers to allergies through eating solid foods, and they have more contact with the wider world and with other children who may be incubating illnesses. So, although the responsibilities of nurseries change with the children, a high level of skilled monitoring, interaction and intervention is still necessary.

SLEEPING AND REST

Nearly all young children need to sleep at some stage during the day and appropriate provision has to be made for this. The arrangements will be different for various age groups, but all will need to feel secure and comfortable in order to drift off to sleep.

Babies should be allowed to follow their natural routine in line with their sleeping patterns at home. Each baby needs to have a cot reserved exclusively for its use. This ensures that the all important sense of continuity for the child can be maintained. It also reduces the possibilities of contracting infections from other children. Regular laundering of sheets and blankets as well as wiping down the cots with disinfectant on a weekly basis are important hygiene standards. If it is necessary for babies enrolled on a part-time basis to share cots, this should be explained carefully to the parents and the procedures for continuity and hygiene followed to the letter. It is preferable for the cots to be in a separate sleeping area, which is regularly monitored at 10- or 15-minute intervals by the staff.

Once children reach the age of two (and above) they should be following the nursery routine. Rest mattresses placed on the floor, with individually labelled sheets and blankets, are the usual provision made for rest times. Hygiene standards must be followed, including ensuring that sheets and blankets are not shared, are washed frequently, and that rest mats are regularly wiped with disinfectant. A comfortable, quiet, warm place which is free from draughts should be provided. Adult company and monitoring need to be provided too, to give children the security to go off to sleep and to wake up reassured.

SKIN CARE

Skin care features in a number of aspects of child health, such as nappy sores, various types of rashes, conditions such as eczema, chapped faces, insect bites and the cuts and grazes arising from active play. It is also an important feature of looking after children of African, Caribbean or Asian origin, because, from birth, black skin and hair should be protected from dryness.

Nurseries are advised to have discussions regularly with parents about the choices of products to use. There are issues about potential allergic reactions, the need to use creams supplied only on a GP prescription and personal preferences. While the nursery should have a range of standard products available, individual parents may wish to supply their own. For example, there is a choice of using petroleum jelly, cocoa butter or perfumed oils to care for black skin and there are cultural and family differences which influence what is appropriate for an individual child.

In addition, nursery staff should be careful not to overlook the preventative action needed to protect children's skin from the detrimental effects of sun. Even on relatively dull days it is probably wise to use sun protection preparations. In the summer, particular attention should be paid to the amount of time which children spend in the sun; only a few minutes of exposure without adequate protection can be too much. Activities in the paddling pool are great fun in good weather, but the routine must include arrangements for appropriate protection. Sun block should always be applied thoroughly and hats worn. This applies to all children including those who are of African or Asian origin. Older children can begin to learn about the necessity of protecting themselves and how to behave sensibly in the sun.

PERSONAL HYGIENE

Personal hygiene habits should be encouraged from a very young age. As soon as the first molars are through, tooth brushing should begin. From the stage of starting potty training children need to be taught how to wash their hands thoroughly, especially whenever they visit the toilet and also after playing outside or handling pets and before meals.

A child's control of the bowel and bladder functions takes some time, and adult assistance, to develop. Each child has to be encouraged to take an appropriate level of responsibility for their toileting and should be helped to develop a regular routine. They will particularly need support on how to cope with 'accidents', constipation, etc.

In general terms, the older the child, the less practical help they are likely to need. However, the nursery staff will still have to ensure that all children are following the best hygiene standards, monitoring or intervening even when children are old enough to take basic responsibility for themselves. Also communicating with parents is essential in order to maintain a consistent approach at home.

ILLNESSES

In general terms, children who are unwell should not be at nursery. Not only do they need the peace and comfort of home and parental attention, but also other children and adults have to be protected, as much as possible, from infections. Under community and environmental health regulations, children suffering from designated infectious diseases must be excluded. Your local authority registration will include advice about the requirements, indicators and length of exclusions. Any child who falls ill at nursery should be sent home as early as possible with their parent or other carer.

The nursery does have to make some accommodation for children who are not always 'entirely well'. Children with chronic conditions, such as eczema, asthma, sickle cell or thalassaemia, may need special support and care from time to time, but they belong in the nursery just as any child does. Children with an injury to be dressed, a limb in plaster, or just recovering from a spell of sickness will also undoubtedly benefit from the routine and activities offered by the nursery.

Providing a warm, quiet, comfortable place for children to sit or rest is a must. Allocating time for a member of staff to specifically monitor, support and care for the child is also essential.

Because partnerships undoubtedly must extend to health matters, liaison with parents and any health professionals working with their children should be given a high priority by the nursery.

MEDICINE

You will be required, as part of the registration process, to have a firm policy on giving medicine to children. It is generally recommended that this should only be done where the medicine has been prescribed by a doctor and is given to the nursery, by a parent, in its original packaging showing the chemist's label, date and recommended dosage. Parents should also be expected to provide their own written instructions and consent for the nursery to administer the medicine. In addition, they should be expected to agree to ensure that doses to be given at home are carried out as prescribed.

When parents ask that patent medicines, herbal preparations, etc. should be dispensed, you will need to have a thorough discussion and reach an understanding with them. You should always reserve the right to say no. However, in many instances, such as relief for teething or eczema, it is likely to be in the child's best interests to say yes. Written instructions and consent from parents are always needed, whatever the circumstances.

Staff and parents probably need to discuss the best strategies for obtaining the child's co-operation in taking medicine. Remember, children may be frightened or simply be determined not to take the medicine!

Medicine Record Sheet

NURSERY

NAME OF CHILD

DATE	TIME	MEDICINE	DOSE	INITIALS	MANAGER'S SPOT CHECK

PARENT'S INSTRUCTIONS

Medication to be given

Dosage

Duration of treatment

Reason for medication

Other details

I request the nursery to give my child the medication which I have provided as indicated above.

Signed   Date

Name

Example of a medicine record sheet

Diet, nutrition and mealtimes

Whatever their age, it is likely that the children attending a nursery each day will be eating the majority of their meals there. Children need to drink and eat regularly throughout the day in order to take in all the nourishment and fluids they need for health and growth. Nutrients are also an important aid to the immune system. Usually nurseries have to provide breakfast, a cooked lunch and a substantial tea as well as drinks and light snacks in the morning and afternoon. This is in addition to bottles for babies, which are best given on demand.

The nursery has a key responsibility to meet the children's nutritional needs as well as to honour individual and family dietary requirements. It is likely that some children attending the nursery may be allergic to certain foods or ingredients, such as cow's milk, nuts or wheat. Some children will have dietary restrictions because of their families' religious beliefs. Other families may want their children to follow a vegetarian regime. In order to make the necessary plans to meet the special requirements of individual children, nurseries need to ask each parent for the relevant information and to review that information regularly.

Understanding that there are serious implications of allergies to soya products and nuts (which may be hidden in foods such as ice cream) is important in making choices about menus and purchasing food. Sound advice from a dietician or a qualified cook is invaluable for generally establishing balanced menus and offering suitable choices and options for the equal benefit of all the children attending the nursery.

BOTTLE FEEDING BABIES

Organisation for bottle feeding babies involves several considerations. There must be suitable facilities and equipment including a sink, refrigerator, kettle, steriliser and a selection of bottles (preferably the babies' own). The 'who and when' of making up bottles has to be planned as part of the routine. Decisions about when to supplement bottle feeds with bottles of water or well diluted baby drinks need to be agreed with parents.

Hygiene and health requirements must be fully understood and scrupulously followed. This includes: thorough hand washing by staff; adequate cleaning of bottles, teats, bottle brushes, etc. to avoid bacterial infections; accuracy in mixing formulae milk and in diluting fruit juices; always using boiled water (which has been cooled); storing prepared bottles in a well regulated refrigerator; throwing away any leftovers and the contents of unused bottles.

Some mothers may prefer to express their milk or to make up bottles at home. The nursery's support for this choice will benefit the care relationship.

FULL DIETS

When children are between four and six months old, solid foods can usually begin to be introduced to their diet. By the age of two years, children will, more or less, eat the same style of diet as an adult. All the main nutritional and health issues apply. For example, a two year old needs to consume 2 pints of fluid, such as juice or water, each day. Of particular significance for young children are: a balanced diet, including whole milk (not skimmed or reduced fat); the use of fresh foods, especially fruit and vegetables; the avoidance of salt, sugar, preservatives, whole nuts and processed (convenience) foods. Although some frozen foods may be suitable, generally the food served in a nursery should be prepared fresh daily.

MEALTIMES

Arrangements for mealtimes (and times for snacks) should take into account the importance of promoting the social and co-ordination skills which children need to acquire, as well as the possible opportunities for developing children's confidence and self-esteem.

Babies need to be held and talked to attentively by a familiar adult. Toddlers need to be given sufficient time and help by the adults to explore their food, attempt to feed themselves and to interact with other children sharing the mealtime. Older children need to be encouraged to help to serve themselves and each other, to use a knife and fork appropriately and to chat sociably.

Whatever the children's age, or degree of 'faddy' eating habits, they will respond positively to attractively presented food, choices and small manageable portions. Mealtimes should be leisured and enjoyable, with no undue pressure placed on children to eat when they are not hungry or on those who take an active dislike to particular foods.

Menus for mealtimes should take account of seasonal variations, the need to introduce children to new textures and flavours and the inclusion of foods from a variety of cultures and cooking styles. Different occasions demand different foods. For example, picnics during outings, tea in the garden, birthday parties and Chinese new year celebrations are all opportunities to extend the range and style of foods to be eaten.

The learning programme can also be usefully linked to meals and snacks. For example, the children may be involved in preparing finger foods, or baking, or growing food which can be eaten later. There are many variations to try.

Conclusion

Children's physical, emotional and social development go hand in hand with their educational progress. These must be given the highest priority in nursery provision. Considerable skill and knowledge is needed to support children's physical and emotional well being. Consequently, appropriately experienced staff are essential to ensuring good outcomes. The staff team should build on the caring role of parents and incorporate each parent's unique knowledge of and preferences for their child.

Initially, basic advice on health, hygiene and nutrition should be sought from local authority sources and external experts. This is particularly important if a nursery is offering places to babies. Reading through a range of the most well regarded books on child development, health and nutrition will be beneficial. Good bookstores and voluntary organisations, including the National Children's Bureau and the Food Commission, can sell and recommend suitable literature.

CHECKLIST

- Policies and practices guidelines
- Childcare and nursery ethos
- Shared care with parents
- Children's emotional development
- Children's social development
- Children's physical development
- Care of babies
- Care of toddlers
- Care of the over-threes
- Confidentiality
- Key worker system
- Settling in period
- Managing children's behaviour
- Child protection
- Daily arrival ad collection of children
- Nursery outings
- Skin and hair care
- Children's personal hygiene
- Children's illnesses
- Children with special health care needs
- Administration of medicines
- Diet, nutrition and menus
- Organisation of mealtimes

10 THE LEARNING PROGRAMME

> When the first baby laughed for the first time, the laugh broke into a thousand pieces and they all went skipping about and that was the beginning of fairies.
>
> J.M. Barrie

This chapter highlights the major issues and complexities related to what and how children learn at nursery. It is a broad subject which nursery providers will have to research in depth on an ongoing basis.

Throughout the chapter there is a deliberate avoidance of terminology such as education, curriculum and teaching. This is to reinforce the message that didactic methods and props such as desks, worksheets, notebooks and homework are not generally appropriate for young children's learning programmes. If they are to have a role it has to be managed with great sensitivity and from a well informed perspective. Most early years educators recommend opportunities for self-directed learning, nurturing of imagination, creativity and love of learning for its own sake, as fundamentals for the development of foundation skills for life.

A lifetime of learning is what one generally expects to prepare children for and it is this preparation you are taking on responsibility for when establishing a full nursery programme. Consequently, a continuous search for deeper understandings of how children learn best and new ideas for enriching the learning opportunities to be offered to all children are part and parcel of the responsibility of running a nursery.

Age differences

As learning begins at birth, it is highly important that education is incorporated into all aspects of nursery life. However, the key to providing adequately for children is to strike a sensible balance between the care and the learning elements of the nursery programme and to have regard for the whole child as well as the varying stages of development of each individual child.

BABIES

Babies, most obviously, require a lot of attention to their physical well-being. However, their capacity for learning and their need to be stimulated cannot be overlooked. Adults talking to the babies, responding to their sounds, singing songs, playing peekaboo games and using repetitive language help babies to learn communication skills and begin to make sense of the world. Stacking boxes, treasure baskets and musical mobiles are examples of early toys which enhance interactions between adults and children as well as providing opportunities for babies to control their own stimulation.

EARLY TODDLERS

Early toddlers need a range of opportunities to explore their environment and the physical world to the full extent allowed by their developmental stage. They benefit from conversation, songs, interactive play, reciprocal responses from adults, social opportunities to interact with other children, building up a circle of friends and familiar routine. Push/pull toys, collections of smallish objects and containers for heuristic play, corn flour and water activities are the tools needed for play and for extending learning.

OLDER TODDLERS

Older toddlers are usually ready and able to experiment with a wide range of opportunities to test out their developing skills. The support of a special adult is critical, especially in recognising the level of security, encouragement and challenge needed. Individual differences in skills and interests are of significance. Hence the particular need for interventions at appropriate times from adults who know each child well. Because of the children's generally short attention span, and their need for a variety of experiences, there has to be a number of options for children to pursue at any one time of the day. Sand, water, paint, crayons, implements for early mark making, large construction toys, picture books and low-level climbing apparatus are just some of the appropriate pieces of equipment. Playing co-operatively with other children and learning to take turns are important too.

OVER THREES

Three to five year olds certainly need a lot of affectionate support, guidance and understanding, however capable and independent they may seem. Their maturation and learning progress depends on this. Adult conversation and interaction should help to develop the reasoning powers of the children. Questioning is as important as demonstrating in extending children's thinking.

It is also important to allow children time, space and opportunities for self-expression and experimentation. Children may concentrate on one activity for long periods of time. They may undertake activities alone or with one or two other children and develop elaborate rules for their games. They should, throughout the day, be in a rich environment, with all the equipment and play settings that it is possible to provide, e.g. sand, musical instruments, art materials, home corner, dressing up clothes, construction toys, puzzles etc. Outings, regular trips to local shops and services, visits to fire stations, museums, city farms, the theatre, parks and markets, etc. will extend the children's curiosity and understanding. That vital 'disposition to learn' can be instilled in children and all the early skills which form the basis of competence in maths, science, language, reading and writing can be enhanced.

How children learn

How children learn is as important as what they learn. As well as considering the significance of developmental stages for children's skills enhancement and acquisition of knowledge, you also need to take account of the process of learning, as well as the role of adults, and the children themselves, in that process.

Children's early learning is determined to a large extent by their physical and emotional development. For example, general growth rates, the development of eye muscles and the abandoning of comfort items, all impinge on the acquisition of skills such as pencil control, recognition of letters, or expressing an idea.

Child psychologists agree that play is an essential part of the process because learning takes place through direct experiences in meaningful contexts. Playing allows children the opportunities they need to use all their senses, construct, explore, discover, create and imagine. Having direct access to equipment, making choices, sharing ideas with other children and with special adults all contribute to learning. Reasonably open-ended play opportunities support children to interact with other children to enrich their experience. Children of mixed ages and abilities playing together learn from each other and share their strengths, ideas and knowledge.

Recently developed understandings of schemas provide insights into what concepts are being developed by a particular child at a particular time. A schema is defined as being an observable repeated pattern of behaviour which may manifest itself through various stages – motor, symbolic, functional dependence- leading to thought. Some common schemas include transporting, wrapping, rotation and ordering. Recognition and understanding of schemas allow adults to plan suitable experiential activities which will further children's conceptual development.

THE ADULT ROLE

The role of adults is significant in children's learning. The learning process is strengthened and enriched when the adult acts as facilitator, planner, motivator, stimulator, enabler, assessor, friend and helpmate. Adults have a responsibility to act as role models, to engage in challenging discussions with children and to encourage children to enjoy a wide range of play activities. They should ensure that there are opportunities for children to extend periods of concentration, persevere with difficult tasks, repeat activities, consolidate their skills and knowledge base, recreate their experiences and observations and to express themselves through a variety of media.

VALUING CHILDREN

Self-esteem is a cornerstone to learning. Each child in the nursery should know that they are valued and respected for their unique contribution to the group. Pleasant, enjoyable days will enhance the children's learning. A caring, happy, child-centred ethos must be integral to the management of the nursery in order to foster the children's full development.

Alongside this there must be recognition that all individuals experience a range of needs and emotions. Learning takes place in different ways depending on the emotions being experienced. Children should be helped to understand their emotions and the nursery environment should offer a range of quiet and noisy activities as well as opportunities for children to play alone or as part of a larger group.

Deciding on the type of learning programme

Those independent schools for which your nursery may be a feeder, your Local Education Authority and OFSTED all have formal expectations of your nursery's

	High Scope	Montessori	Steiner
Specific staff qualification	No	Yes	No
Specific training needed	Yes	Yes	Yes
Special equipment needed	No	Yes	No
Particular daily routine	Yes	No	Yes
Particular teaching methods	Yes	Yes	Yes
Own terminology	Yes	Yes	Yes
Particular method of grouping children	Yes	No	No
Particular room layout	Yes	No	No

Comparison of some learning systems

learning programme and the skills and knowledge which children should have acquired by the time they reach compulsory school age. The choices to make and deciding how to integrate the sometimes confusing requirements or advice are testing. Sensitivity to children's needs for intellectual development, your philosophical preferences and lessons from research should be the key factors in determining the form of learning programme for your nursery. Notwithstanding your decisions, you must also take on board the values of the nursery staff and the expectations of the parents. Particular attention has to be given to ensuring that the final result is coherent, balanced and consistent.

THE CHOICES

There are a variety of accepted early years philosophies or educational systems which are worth exploring before making final decisions about the programme to be followed in your nursery.

The programme most usually found in British nursery schools is an eclectic model which incorporates aspects of a range of philosophies and psychological concepts. There is a strong influence from educators such as Maria Montessori, Margaret Macmillan, Jean Piaget and Jerome Bruner. The programme is further influenced by the expectations of the National Curriculum (intended for school age children), the recently established Desirable Learning Outcomes and current academic thinking.

The alternative programmes, to a greater or lesser extent, are fixed and tied to one particular philosophy or method of practice. The most well established and widely recognised systems are High Scope, Montessori and Steiner (see the comparison on p. 129). They each have an organisation and body of literature to train staff, to explain their ideas and to promote their way of doing things.

Making a choice is highly important. Whichever approach you decide to follow, you can be certain that it will dictate some particularly significant parameters such as your own learning curve, recruitment of staff and selection of equipment. Business competition issues may also be of significance. What are parents seeking? What are other nurseries offering? As the saying goes, the choice is yours, but it should not be made blindly!

GOOD PRACTICE ISSUES

When you begin to determine the learning programme for your nursery, whatever philosophy or framework you adopt, due consideration should also be given to a number of contingent issues which impact on practice.

- A key objective for any learning programme has to be to ensure that all children gain the skills of reasoning, observing, questioning, researching, responding and expressing themselves in a clear and positive way. These form the basic skills on which future learning is founded.
- Balance is essential. All the possible opportunities for learning should be included and accorded equal importance. For example, both reality and fantasy are significant; so too are adult direction and children's independent

Any tendency to place exclusive emphasis on the 3Rs should be curbed

activity. Children need both physical exercise and table top activities. They need to experience participating in large groups and small groups as well as playing alone.

- Any tendency to place almost exclusive emphasis on the '3Rs', or knowledge of subjects related to adult pastimes (e.g. opera, politics, sport) should be curbed. To support the natural and appropriate developmental and learning process, children need a very wide range of opportunities and experiences. Children also need well-rounded programmes to find their own particular ways to excel.
- Respect for the values of equality of opportunity regardless of gender, ability and ethnic origin must be built into the daily activities. An understanding of the wider community's religious beliefs, languages and cultural traditions should also be included. It is important for all the nursery staff to consciously avoid perpetuating stereotyped images and ideas. Staff must have a personal commitment, understanding and sensitivity to the issues, especially in a community which offers children few opportunities to experience diversity first hand.
- Gender stereotyping should be avoided. Books, dressing up clothes and language should be considered carefully by the adults to ensure that children are not receiving any unduly stereotypical images about their own sex. Boys need to feel comfortable playing with the dolls. Girls need to feel that a toy hammer and nails can be used to help them to create something useful.
- Nurseries need to acknowledge the parent's fundamental role in their child's education. This involves nurturing links between home and nursery, inviting parents to join in with nursery activities and making opportunities for

parents to share information and observations about their child. Parents should be given information about general policies, the arrangements for the learning programme and the overall objectives. They also need to be kept informed, both informally and formally – by both verbal and written means, of their child's activities and achievements.

These good practice issues all have practical implications. They should be reflected in the nursery's policies and in the planning of the care and learning programmes. They also impact on the selection of staff and the choice of equipment, books, posters, display materials, etc.

Organising the resources

Resources represent a major cost in the nursery business plan, but they are essential for the children's learning programme. Maximising the value of your resources is key to an effective learning programme. It is useful to remember that resources include staff, space, equipment, community opportunities and, perhaps, external experts.

STAFF

Of course the most valuable, and the most expensive, resource is the staff team. Choosing staff who will work well with children is the first organisational requirement. However, this is not the only requirement. The working environment should be conducive to staff giving of their best, planning together, sharing skills and supporting each other as a real team. Staff need ready access to the provision of early years information, reference books, additional training and opportunities for professional development. Working in isolation does not develop resources. There should be opportunities for staff to visit and learn about other types of practice, make links with other local children's services and to attend conferences, exhibitions, etc.

PREMISES

The significance of the appropriate use and role of indoor space is usually well understood through consideration of the basic requirements of the care and learning programme. However, to make best use of the premises does take planning.

When choosing equipment, storage furniture and soft furnishings, for example, proportions and quantity are important considerations. Areas to be used by children have to be arranged to allow plenty of free floor space to accommodate more than one big activity at a time. Thought has to be given to the lighting, acoustics, floor coverings, etc. to allow for the full range of activities – including quiet, messy, construction, table top, small group and large group – which may all be taking place at the same time. Rooms dedicated to only one or two types of activities may work against the learning programme by limiting children's choices and initiative. How children and staff will access all the facilities which might be needed during the day, such as storage areas, toilets and changes of clothing have significance for the learning programme too.

The significance and role of the outdoor space is all too frequently misunderstood or even ignored. Outdoor areas can be a valuable and integral part of the learning environment. Of course the outside play areas are appropriate places for children to work off their exuberance and develop their large motor skills, co-ordination, etc. Nevertheless, outside play opportunities should offer more than this. Structured activities based on the natural world (including birds, insects, plants and trees) offer children opportunities to observe, question, and experience wonder. Games such as throwing balls or playing hopscotch can incorporate mathematical concepts. Many songs, stories and imaginative activities have an added dimension if they take place out of doors.

SYSTEMS FOR SPECIFIC SKILLS

Commercially developed learning systems, such as those for early reading and mathematics, can sometimes be appropriate. Many are advertised and reviewed in childcare and education magazines. However, most schemes are fairly rigid and require a high level of adult direction and recording, so they can be difficult to combine with nursery learning themes and cross-curricular methods. There is also a danger that staff, parents and managers may be lulled into complacency rather than actively planning for children's learning. Reliance on a full programme of pre-printed worksheets and workbooks is not what early years education standards are meant to be about; remember the requirements of individual needs, the development of imagination and the support of confident forms of self-expression. If you do decide to use one of these systems, it is important to select a package which suits your nursery and to ensure that all staff are appropriately trained in its use. The skills to be learned through the packaged system also have to be integrated into the full nursery programme in the usual way. So, for example, development of literacy skills still has to be included in the planning for the home corner, story time, nursery displays, etc.

Desirable Learning Outcomes for four year olds

In 1996 the Office for Standards in Education (OFSTED) and the School Curriculum and Assessment Authority (SCAA) developed a set of Desirable Outcomes for Children's Learning. Their existence and use are linked to the system for nurseries claiming the Nursery Education Grant. Whilst these Desirable Learning Outcomes are targeted at four year olds, they do offer good signposts for the general organisation of the progression of nursery learning programmes for all age groups.

The Desirable Learning Outcomes are intended for use across all sectors of provision (private, voluntary and statutory) and are designed to be broad enough to encompass all accepted approaches to early years learning (High Scope, Montessori, etc.). The objective is to ensure that every four year old child has an equal foundation on which to build later educational achievement.

There are six designated Areas of Learning. Each encompasses a number of different groups of Desirable Learning Outcomes:

- Personal and Social Development
- Language and Literacy
- Mathematics
- Knowledge and Understanding of the World
- Physical Development
- Creative Development.

More information about the Desirable Learning Outcomes is contained in OFSTED publications.

Children with special educational needs

All children are individual and are likely to have some special needs at one time or another during their childhood. However, there are children who have longer term, serious and particular special needs. These may be related to:

- physical disabilities
- medical conditions
- sensory impairments
- learning difficulties
- gifted learning abilities
- emotional or behavioural problems.

Best practice in childcare has traditionally placed an emphasis on integrating young children with special needs into mainstream services – more recently begun to be regarded as 'inclusion'. It is expected that good nurseries have enrolment policies which welcome all children and, in the spirit of offering equal opportunities, ensure that every child is valued and treated with respect. Providing opportunities for every child to develop to their full potential must be a matter of principle. All children benefit from making friends, learning self-control, increasing their self-confidence, developing literacy and numeracy skills, and discovering how to interact appropriately with adults and children outside their family group.

The main practical implications of enrolling children with special needs in the nursery are related to the facilities offered within the premises, the staffing levels, the opportunities for staff training and the links to be developed with outside agencies, including voluntary organisations. Each child with special needs will require a different set of resources. With the help of parents it should be possible to identify what is required before enrolment and to review this at regular intervals as the child progresses.

THE CODE OF PRACTICE

The Education Act 1989 addressed some of the special needs issues. This was followed by The Code of Practice on the Identification and Assessment of Special Educational Needs 1994, which sets out good practice and a five-stage Model for Assessment.

The first three stages are based on the responsiveness of staff, with the consent and involvement of parents. They include an initial identification that a child may have some degree of special educational need, the gathering of relevant information and the seeking of external specialist assistance. The other two stages involve the Local Education Authority in arranging a formal assessment which may lead on to Statementing.

It is intended that through applying the Code of Practice it may be possible to begin to address special needs at an early age, for the benefit of the children involved. Consequently, it is now expected that all nurseries, in whatever sector, will follow the Code of Practice. In fact, nurseries in receipt of Nursery Education Grant are required to adopt the Code.

Children for whom English is an additional language

Children whose first language is not English are not classed as having special educational needs. Nevertheless, there has to be regular and thoughtful planning in order for them to benefit from the learning programme. This should be designed to enable them to progress developmentally and to be integrated with the whole group of children attending the nursery, while their language skills and understanding of English are strengthened.

However, it is important that in the baby and toddler stages these children are assisted by their parents, and the nursery, to initially progress in their home language. This is because they will need a fundamental grasp of their home language before they embark on learning English as an additional language.

All children's language and literacy skills are best enhanced through a cross-curricular approach which covers every area of development. This method is particularly helpful for EAL (ESL) children. It is also important for their general development and self-esteem that the nursery ensures that there are appropriate resources, displays, books and music, etc. which positively reflect their home culture including their written and spoken language.

The learning programme from the children's perspective

How the routine for the day is organised and the way the learning programme is structured are matters which need to be considered from the children's perspective. Within the plan for each day there must be scope and flexibility to allow for the children's input. Babies should be able to follow their natural, individual rhythms of waking, sleeping, feeding. Older children should be able to make choices, pursue an absorbing activity and explore current enthusiasms, particular friendships, or unexpected anxieties.

Children's rights to make choices must be accommodated. Opportunities can be structured into the daily plans for children to choose types of play and equipment, to direct their own time, to be in charge of what they are doing, and to extend or amend an adult initiated activity. How far this independence can be encouraged is really only limited by the maturity of the children and the closing time of the nursery. The degree to which adult interventions are sensible or acceptable should be judged by the extent to which they enhance the children's enjoyment or understanding and are welcomed by the children.

If children feel that they are respected as individuals, that they are valued, that their efforts are acknowledged and praised, then their confidence will grow. It will also grow if they can test out their skills, be appreciated by their peers and undertake manageable responsibilities including those of choosing and tidying away play equipment. Self-confidence and self-esteem are key to the learning process.

Planning for children's learning

Whichever philosophies or concepts of learning and curriculum you decide to adopt, you will need to make them operational. This involves planning. A sensible practice is to plan, well in advance, and in general terms, to have a framework for a specified block of time, perhaps a month or even half a term. There may even be a 'grand plan' or curriculum, which provides a cycle for a whole year, to be repeated each year. Longer term plans have to be supplemented with shorter term plans for each day and each week. This is not intended to be detrimental to spontaneity, but to be supportive of ensuring balance, continuity and coherent progress in the children's learning process.

To be effective, the plans have to ensure that you are using all your resources appropriately, addressing the needs of the children enrolled and that they fit with knowledge of how children learn and the philosophy being adopted by the nursery. They should offer a shape to the day and the week which will offer children a wide variety of experiences and support your programme objectives. Staff skills and roles underpin all this and consequently staff must be closely involved in, if not directing, the planning.

Plans should be kept on file for future reference, and for monitoring and evaluation at staff meetings. They are essential tools for monitoring your planning process and for assessing the general effectiveness of your practice. It is useful to refer to plans when trying to identify any weaknesses in how children are grouped, arrangements for use of resources, staff preparations, equipment needed and adult understandings of the learning objectives intended.

WRITTEN FORMATS

Plans should be in writing, so that they can be referred to by everyone involved, especially staff members who have to prepare appropriately for each day. To be useful, the plans should always be available for easy reference by staff during the day. In addition to being posted in the main children's activity areas, they should

Weekly Learning Plan					
Dates:					
Theme:					
Age group:					
Areas of learning	Monday	Tuesday	Wednesday	Thursday	Friday
Personal and social	Intended learning outcome				
	Activity				
Language and literacy					
Mathematics					
Knowledge and understanding of the world					
Physical development					
Creative development					

Example of a planning matrix

be kept at various other places in the nursery such as in the store cupboards, manager's office, staff room and on the parents' notice board. Parents and professional visitors will also need to see and understand the plans in order to assure themselves of how children's progress is intended to take shape.

Detailed weekly and daily plans are probably best presented in chart form. They should include headings for each Area of Learning and indicate the purpose or intended outcome of each activity, linked to the Desirable Learning Outcomes as appropriate. Plans should incorporate separate learning objectives for each age group. Which members of staff will be involved, which pieces of equipment will be used, how much time will be required, how children will be grouped and what line of questioning will be used to extend learning, should all be indicated by notation on the plan. Supplementary plans and charts can be used to indicate room layout for specific indoor activities or events and layout for the outdoor activities.

A THEMATIC PEG

One of the most widely adopted approaches to planning is to use a topical theme as the framework – a peg on which to hang the chosen learning outcomes. A new theme may be followed each month, or one theme may continue for a longer period (e.g. a whole term), with sub-themes introduced on a weekly basis. The theme determines which activities, decor, displays, social activities, songs and stories are to be introduced to the children. Within the plan for the theme, the educational objectives for each area of learning should be set out clearly.

Additionally, a cross-curricular approach may be used to pursue learning objectives. For example, there is much scope for mathematics in art – shape, size, dimensions, pattern, vicinity, perspective, time, space. There is also quite a lot of scope for the development of literacy through art – mark making, control of pencils or brushes, direction and narrative illustration.

Monitoring and assessing children's progress

It is not possible to discuss a learning programme without addressing the subject of the monitoring and assessment of each child's development. This is best accomplished through regular observations of the children and regular collection of examples of the children's work (paintings, mark making, charts, tape recordings of songs or story telling). The children themselves as well as parents and other carers should all be invited to contribute to the process in order to have a well-rounded view of each child.

Ultimately, shared assessment information can provide a useful link between nursery, home, first schools and health services. There are resulting benefits in terms of a more holistic knowledge of children and opportunities for adults to help children build on existing skills and knowledge. Some form of assessment summary, to be given to parents, is particularly valuable and of significance when children are leaving the nursery.

It is possible to use any number of systems or combination of systems for monitoring and assessment. Observation by adults is the key and observations may be either random as noticed, timed as a snapshot, or based on specific tasks set for the children. Some account must be taken of the accepted developmental milestones and many assessment or profiling systems incorporate a method of charting individual children against generalised benchmarks for their age. The formats for record keeping may be checklists, open narrative or brief notation under headings, plus collections of examples of the children's work.

Whatever approach is taken to assessment, it is more helpful to children if records present a positive image of what the child can do. Always bear in mind the importance of self-esteem and the fact that individual differences are quite pronounced in the under-eights.

USEFUL RECORDS

The significance of monitoring/assessment is that it provides the nursery staff with a systematic way of identifying children's individual strengths and weaknesses. The strengths can be reinforced and the skills or knowledge areas which need to be supported or challenged can be made a focus for planning. Monitoring and assessment systems are particularly helpful with identifying special needs – some as straightforward as recognising the abilities of a shy child or the insecurities of a particularly verbal child. Such systems also ensure that part-time children in the nursery, who can all too easily be overlooked, are catered for.

Conclusion

The learning programme goes hand in hand with good childcare, whatever the child's age. Together they form the most significant focus for a nursery. Careful, child-centred planning and assessment, within a suitable framework, are essential to ensure that the learning curriculum will be effective and will help children to achieve their full potential.

Useful guidance on learning programmes and resources should be available from your Local Education Authority or your local Early Years Registration and Inspection Unit. The Office for Standards in Education (OFSTED) and the Department for Education and Employment (DfEE) publish documents relating to the Desirable Learning Outcomes for children of nursery age and the National Curriculum. Magazines and newspapers such as *Nursery World*, *Child Education* and the *Times Education Supplement*, provide a host of ideas and consideration of current issues. There is a large amount of information to absorb and wide reading is recommended.

CHECKLIST

Age groups
Separate programmes and planning for:
- babies
- early toddlers
- older toddlers
- three to five year olds.

CHECKLIST continued

Approaches
Choices to be made from possible programmes:
- mainstream, broad based
- High Scope
- Montessori
- Steiner.

Resources
Planned best use of:
- staff
- premises – indoor and outdoor
- equipment.

OFSTED and SCAA requirements and guidance
- Code of Practice for Children with Special Needs
- Desirable Learning Outcomes

Six Areas of Learning:
- Personal and Social Development
- Language and Literacy
- Mathematics
- Knowledge and Understanding of the World
- Physical Development
- Creative Development.

Good practice issues
Consider:
- developmental differences
- individual needs
- balanced programme
- valuing children
- skills for learning for life
- planning
- equality
- parental involvement
- monitoring
- assessment
- record keeping.

PART C
Monitoring for success

This section covers a range of issues which you will need to address on an on-going basis as you manage your nursery. The subjects are diverse, but in many ways emphasise the linkages between childcare and business issues. This is especially evident in the last two chapters which focus on the relationship with parents and the setting and maintenance of appropriate quality standards in your nursery.

When monitoring how your nursery operates, you should not overlook any of the aspects of starting and managing a nursery covered in the first two sections. Whether childcare or business matters, they will all evolve over time and require review, reflection and replanning from time to time.

11 HUMAN RESOURCES AND EMPLOYMENT

> **What this chapter covers:**
> - **The importance of staffing matters**
> - **The legal context**
> - **Planning for employment**
> - **The recruitment process**
> - **Selecting staff**
> - **Contracts of employment**
> - **Employer's obligations**
> - **Keeping the employment relationship going**
> - **Interviews as part of the employment framework**

It is immoral to misuse people, under use them and abuse them, but it is highly moral to call forth and make use of the talents that are in people. It is also certain that people will not use their gifts to the benefits of the organisation unless they are treated as people with all the needs that people have.

St Thomas Aquinas

This chapter puts forward the essential elements involved in employing nursery staff. It is an important subject because the success of a nursery depends to a large extent on the staff. Their attitudes and actions set the tone for the nursery. Their practices reflect the underlying quality standards of the care provision. Staff also impact significantly on the budget and business plan. Recruitment, employment and training costs are a key item of expenditure. Consequently, a nursery must make every effort, through its employment and human resource practices, to ensure a high level of commitment from staff, to retain the same staff for more than a few years and to build a strong reputation for the nursery based on the professional standards demonstrated by the staff team.

The importance of staffing matters

It should be noted that from a childcare perspective, the knowledge, qualities and experience of staff are of key importance. Whatever else the nursery may offer, it is the individual professional carers who impact directly on the children and inspire confidence in parents. Staff methods and relationships with the children and parents have a major effect on the outcomes for the children. Therefore, recruiting and retaining talented staff, who genuinely like and understand children, is a must, if the nursery is to offer a service which can benefit children.

Striving to be a good employer is the key to good human resources management. This must encompass following the regulations laid down in employment law, having a positive attitude to staff matters, applying the ethics of equality and fair play, respecting the staff as individuals and generally taking a professional, businesslike approach. Reliance on good will, casual promises for the future, friendships, etc. is unlikely to meet legal obligations, and is certainly not practical, even for a small nursery.

The legal context

Employers have to comply with specific legal duties to act responsibly and reasonably within the framework of employment law. Employees' rights and employers' responsibilities can be complicated and there are heavy penalties for improper actions by employers. Legislation is designed to protect the employee. Compliance can appear to be difficult and to work against the employer's interests. However, if employers aim to be fair and caring, the essence of the requirements will usually be immediately comprehensible.

The legal dimension covers virtually every aspect of employment. This includes transfer of business undertakings, insolvency, redundancy, dismissal, discipline, grievances, trade union membership, sickness, maternity benefits, health and safety, discrimination on grounds of sex, race or disability, competence and fitness for work.

Law is generally a complex matter and especially so when it comes to employment. Employment matters are governed by more than a dozen pieces of legislation as well as updated regulations, a considerable amount of case law and several Codes of Practice. It is essential to have access to reliable employment law and personnel advice. Guidance should be sought and followed carefully, from the minute you begin to plan employing staff.

Planning for employment

Before starting the recruitment process, it is essential to develop a realistic model of the staff team to be employed. This has to include all the factors, such as how many staff, with what qualifications, working what hours, for what rates of pay and benefits, following what job descriptions and being managed in what manner. Consultation with your financial and legal advisers should inform the process of building your model in order to ensure that it is financially and legally viable.

STAFF EXPERIENCE AND QUALIFICATIONS

An early priority is to find out what the local authority requirements are with regard to staffing. What percentage of the staff must be qualified? Which qualifications are recognised? What length of experience is expected for the manager? What are the requirements for the 'fit person'? What checks will have to be carried out? How long will this take? Can staff be employed conditionally prior to the receipt of the results of the local authority checks? How many members of staff will need to have an up-to-date, full, first aid certificate? Which first aid certificates are recognised? Do the cook and manager have to hold food handling qualifications? What else is required?

The nursery philosophy and management plans will suggest some additional requirements. Are staff with particular training or qualifications essential? What about Montessori or High Scope training, NVQ Assessor status, knowledge of more than one language, swimming and life saving certificates, or experience of minibus driving? What will each job involve and what skills and personal qualities will be needed within the team? What degree of autonomy is it anticipated that staff will need to exercise?

JOB DESCRIPTIONS AND PERSON SPECIFICATIONS

The next stage is to start to draw up the appropriate documentation to support the recruitment process. This will essentially be based on 'job descriptions' and 'person specifications' for each post. These two documents serve as mutual reference points for both the employer and potential employee. A copy of the job description and person specification for each post should be sent out to candidates with the application form.

A job description is a written statement of the duties and responsibilities the employee must undertake as part of their work. It is important to take time to develop the job description because it helps the employer to clarify their expectations and outlines the work for the employee. The job description document may contain some overall objectives as well as specific tasks. Try to describe the tasks in general terms, but do not leave out important areas of responsibility. It is common practice to indicate the job title, weekly hours (usually between 35 and 40 inclusive of lunch breaks) and the line of management responsibility (to whom they report and who reports to them).

A person specification is a statement of the characteristics required for a particular job. It refers to qualifications, experience and particular skills (perhaps linked to children's ages). In drawing up a person specification, those requirements identified initially have to be included and designated as 'essential'. Other factors should be considered for inclusion but be realistically designated as 'desirable'. For reasons of equal opportunities it is crucial that the person specification only includes absolute requirements as 'essential'. By making proper use of written person specifications, the recruitment process is more likely to be fair to all applicants, and to have a generally reliable result.

PAY AND CONDITIONS TO BE OFFERED

Pay rates, benefits and payment systems are important contractual matters. They are of key interest to every employee and have great significance for the nursery management because of the very nature of contractual obligations. The proposed nursery standards, the staffing requirements and the business plan will

Person specification

The following list has been developed to assist in the recruitment of staff for the Nursery. It outlines both the main essential skills and qualities, as well as those which are desirable.

	Essential/Desirable
Childcare skills	
Experience with children under five	E
Experience with babies	E
Group care experience	D
Training to work with children	D
Good practice in and awareness of equality issues	E
Knowledge of Desirable Learning Outcomes	D
First Aid training	D
Experience of planning activities	D
Experience of writing observation and assessment records	E
Personal qualities	
Good health	E
Energy and general enthusiasm	E
Good grooming and personal hygiene	E
Sense of humour	E
Personal maturity	E
Ability to work with other people	E
Positive outlook on life	E
Enjoyment of children	E
Understanding of the needs and expectations of working parents	E
Special talents or interests	D

Example of a person specification

influence the pay and conditions to be offered. However, the minimum level of pay is likely to be dictated by what other nurseries are offering. However, if the nursery is aiming for high quality standards, reminders about peanuts and monkeys, carrots and sticks, gratification and satisfaction, should be heeded!

In deciding on pay and benefits the applicants' points of view must be understood. What is the total package being offered? Is this realistic? Will there be opportunities for professional progress? Will the applicant think the job is worthwhile and a post to which they can make a commitment for a substantial period of time?

SALARIES

When considering individual salaries, factors such as experience and special skills have to be taken into account. An experienced worker will expect a higher rate of pay than someone newly qualified. Generally, employees will expect to be rewarded for loyalty and increasing skills over a period of time. And do not forget about the Equal Pay Act 1970 which means that men and women must receive equal pay and benefits.

Establishing a set of pay scales for each post in the nursery is prudent. Scales can be used to anticipate the nursery budgets for a year in advance and to facilitate regular reviews of pay and benefits. Staff can use them to gauge their position within the overall staffing scene and to plan their own future progression. Pay scales should be applied fairly, should be recorded in a written document and should be known to all staff.

Beyond the basic pay rates, decisions have to be taken on whether or not funding can be committed to pay improvements. These can include: annual increments on the pay scales, regular cost of living increases to upgrade the pay scales, profit-related pay schemes, pay schemes related to child enrolment figures and bonuses at year ends.

BENEFITS

There are tax implications as well as general levels of attractiveness and practicality to be noted when considering other forms of remuneration. However, some possibilities are: living accommodation, use of a car, subsidised workplace childcare and paid study leave.

Benefits such as paid holidays, paid sick days and pensions are fairly standard offerings. They may not be legally required and do have significant cost implications, but remember their importance for maintaining a happy workforce.

The recruitment process

It is crucial to plan ahead so that the nursery has the right team at the right time. In working out a time-scale for staff starting dates you will have to remember to allow sufficient time to draw up all the necessary documents, place advertisements, short-list applicants, arrange interviews and allow for local authority/police checks, etc. It may be helpful to know that a very basic straightforward recruitment process will probably take about 15 weeks if staff have to give notice in an existing job.

It is probably best to develop an application form rather than rely on receiving CVs and letters as expressions of interest. With an application form you can direct applicants to supply precisely the information needed. This is very helpful, e.g. to uncover in-depth information about skills, salary expectations, first aid training, etc. It also helps to ensure that applicants are on an equal footing in terms of presentation of information.

ADVERTISING

Placing of adverts for staff involves some imagination. It is bound to be a relatively expensive process and so there has to be some assurance that the adverts will get the widest coverage and appeal to the appropriate target group. If the budget can be stretched, advertising in more than one publication is recommended.

Local newspapers are an obvious place to advertise, but it would be wise to read a few back editions to ascertain whether or not there is a recognised pattern of advertisements for the type of job being offered and the quality of applicants being sought. If not, think again.

The national press and specialist magazines may be more expensive to advertise in, but they are also more likely to produce a larger selection of suitable applicants.

The national minority ethnic newspapers are frequently also used for recruitment advertising. This is regarded as good practice in equal opportunities terms, because it demonstrates that the job is open to all sectors of the community.

However, wherever advertisements are to be placed, care must be taken with the wording and intent, not to contravene the Sex Discrimination Act 1975, the Race Relations Act 1976 or the Disability Discrimination Act. There are some grounds for exemptions to these Acts, when a 'genuine occupational qualification' is involved. The circumstances under which exemptions apply are quite precise and those nurseries which recognise the need to exercise the exemptions are advised to seek the help of experts at the Equal Opportunities Commission and the Commission for Racial Equality.

The style and size of an advertisement says a lot to potential applicants. It may be seen as an indication of what value is placed on personnel matters and on the nursery's image. Again, it is suggested that a trawl of publications for similar adverts to see what the standard is, will be worthwhile. As a minimum, an advertisement should contain details of the location of the nursery, number and ages of children enrolled, staff working hours, and some description of the type of qualifications and experience required. It may be useful to indicate a closing date for applications or a starting date for work. It is probably in the nursery's best interests to indicate the salary scale range and paid holidays and other benefits. An informative advert should ensure that potentially good applicants will apply and that there are no disappointments or embarrassments in short-listing and interviewing applicants who would not consider an offer because they are seeking a higher salary or longer holidays, etc. This is particularly so in areas where there is an active job market.

OTHER ROUTES

It is possible to combine advertising with the use of Job Centre facilities and recruitment agencies. But do check whether or not other similar jobs have been successfully filled this way and what charges may be incurred!

Word of mouth recruitment is not the best route to putting together an ace team or supporting equality employment standards. However, you may know someone with appropriate skills and experience and in whom you have great faith for getting the nursery off to a good start. Depending on the size of team to be recruited, it could be possible to fill one or two posts using local networks, but posts should still be advertised and all applicants considered before making (even informal) offers.

Selecting staff

Once a number of applications have been received, you can begin the selection process. It is likely that it will be necessary to sift through the applications to draw up a short-list of suitable candidates to invite to interview. The short-listing should be done with reference to the person specification in order to be fair to all applicants. No one should appear on the short list if they fail to meet the person specification and all applicants who fit the person specification should be short listed.

If applicants did not previously receive a statement of details about the nursery and a job description, they should certainly do so when they are invited for an interview. This will help them to prepare and will save you precious time during the interview in answering the inevitable basic questions.

THE SELECTION INTERVIEW

The nursery will need to prepare for the interviews. When and where will they take place? Who will do the interviewing? How can the interview panel implement good equal opportunity practices? Allow at least 30 minutes per candidate. Do not forget to allow some time for lunch or tea. Make sure you build in some flexibility to the schedule for candidates who need to come at some time other than that specified. Will the interview location be difficult to find? Send clear directions and allow some time for candidates who get lost and arrive late.

Each candidate should be given a warm welcome and each should be treated equally. Although individual supplementary questions can be asked in order to draw out information, basically identical questions should be put to each candidate. All candidates should be offered the chance to give more information, to ask questions and to look around the nursery.

Deciding on a set of interview questions can be quite taxing. The questions need to give the candidates opportunities to present themselves at their best. However, it is also necessary to probe for their practical skills and to enquire about any gaps in their employment history. For some posts it may be appropriate to ask candidates (giving them advance notice, of course) to give a presentation or to carry out a demonstration activity. Suggesting that candidates bring portfolios or photographs showing them at work can be helpful to both parties in the interview situation.

It is invaluable to make notes during the interview and to add a written summary or assessment at the end. This helps to refresh the interviewers' memories

INTERVIEW RECORD

Candidate _____

Date of Interview _____ **Interviewers** _____

General points	Other notes
	■ Introduction to post etc.
	■ Opportunity to ask questions
Childcare skills	■ Information on next stage of recruitment
General experience	
Baby experience	
Experience/training for equal opportunities approach	■ Certificates or work examples available
Special interests	
Additional training	■ Holiday plans
First Aid certificate	
Personal qualities	
Motivation	■ Possible starting date
Career goals	
Personality (humour, maturity, outlook, self-reliance)	■ Assessment
Employability (initiative, adaptability, common sense, team work)	
Health record	
Suitability of post	
Hours/shifts, pay expectations	
Understands nature of business	■ Offer
Understands expectations of working parents	
Understands/already follows nursery policies	

Example of an interview record sheet

when choosing between candidates. It highlights areas for further questioning at second interviews. It also means there is a written record of the basis for the decisions taken on selection and this helps protect the nursery from claims of unfair selection procedures.

THE FOLLOW-UP STAGE

After the interviews have all been completed, there comes a follow-up stage. All applicants, whether successful or unsuccessful, deserve a prompt letter to let them know the position. However, it is wise not to turn down second-choice candidates until acceptances have been received from the preferred candidates. Holding letters may be useful.

Making a telephone call to outline the job offer to preferred candidates may be a good idea. Whilst it is legally committing the nursery to a contract, it is an opportunity to test out the likelihood of candidates' accepting the offer, to agree starting dates and holidays to be honoured and to give an indication that references, police checks etc. are about to be taken up. It also opens the door for good communications, which should set the tone for the future employment relationship. The telephone offer should be followed up by a formal written job offer letter.

REFERENCES

References must be taken up. It is usual to request two references (one personal, one related to work or training) for each candidate. Sometimes references are requested to coincide with interviews, but it is common practice to take them up at the time of offering the job.

Request letters should be sent to the referees, indicating what type of information is required (i.e. reliability, health record, skills etc.). Enclosing an envelope may speed up the reply. Testimonials held by the candidate are fine as indicators but they are not the same as a reference. Similarly telephone calls should not replace written responses to the request for a reference.

Police checks on childcare staff are carried out by most local authorities. These checks serve a useful purpose and are good deterrents to unsuitable applicants. However, they have a limited value to the selection process. Frequently there is a long time lag in getting a response. Checks usually focus on convictions rather than charges or suspicions. The police files contain no information about personal qualities, employability, work attendance records or skills with children.

INFORMATION NEEDED FROM NEW EMPLOYEES

In order to move forward with the employment arrangements and to satisfy the local authority requirements, it is necessary to obtain certain information and documentation from new members of staff. It is probably most efficient if the necessary forms and requests for information are included with the offer letter. These include:

- police check forms
- health questionnaire
- proof of relevant professional qualifications
- proof of other qualifications, e.g. First Aid
- details of next of kin
- bank details for payment of salary
- P45 or other tax form
- National Insurance number.

Contracts of employment

Once an offer of employment is made a legal contract exists. A formal offer letter, setting out all the necessary details, should be sent as soon as possible. However, it is prudent to indicate that the offer is subject to receipt of satisfactory references and police checks (and health checks too, if you are requesting them). Asking the new staff member to sign and return a duplicate copy of the offer letter completes the process.

Under the Employment Protection (Consolidation) Act 1978 and the Trade Union Reform and Employment Rights Act 1993 employers are obliged to provide new workers with a written statement of the terms and conditions of employment within two months of the start of employment. The offer letter can be suitable and sufficiently detailed to meet all the requirements. Alternatively you may decide to use a supplementary conditions of service document or staff handbook, or a printed contract of employment form. There are some acceptable commercially developed forms which can be suitable for use. Your solicitor could also help to draw up suitable contract documentation.

THE PRINCIPAL STATEMENT

Whatever format you decide to use, it must be ensured that all the information required by law is provided and that this is done within the specified time-scale of two months. Some information must be provided in a single document or principal statement, such as the offer letter. Other information may be provided in instalments, or in a supplementary document such as a conditions of service document or a staff handbook. In all circumstances, sufficient written detail should be given to make clear what is intended.

The information which must be included in the principal statement is:

- the names of employer and employee
- the date when the period of continuous employment begins
- the scale and rate of remuneration
- the pay intervals (e.g. weekly or monthly)
- the hours of work and normal working hours
- entitlements and arrangements for paid holidays
- job title and brief description of duties
- the place of work.

All the information required by law must be provided

The additional information which must also be given, but which may be provided in instalments, is:

- the length of the notice period
- details about the contracting-out of National Insurance
- details of any collective (trade union) agreement
- conditions relating to sicknesses and sick pay
- conditions relating to pensions
- details of the disciplinary rules
- details of the grievance procedure.

Most nurseries will be employing a sufficient number of staff to be obliged to set out the details of a health and safety policy. Other contractual matters, such as maternity leave, redundancy and retirement, will be assumed to comply with the statutory minimums, unless more generous terms are specified in the conditions of service. To meet nursery registration requirements, it is likely that an equal opportunities policy will be needed.

ADDITIONAL POINTS

Given the nature of nursery work, it is a good idea to include in the conditions of service, references to matters of particular importance. For example, it would be wise to mention:

- the safety and well-being of the children
- reporting of suspected child abuse
- confidentiality
- use of drink or drugs at work
- working under the influence of drink or drugs

- smoking at work
- reporting of notifiable illnesses
- overtime working arrangements
- overtime pay rates and time off in lieu.

It is also useful to supplement the conditions of service with other documents including the detailed job description, pay scales and company policies.

Employer's obligations

There are a number of duties and obligations placed on an employer. Inevitably these obligations have to be backed up by a detailed record keeping system. For example, as part of the Statutory Sick Pay scheme there must be a separate record for each member of staff which shows all their sickness absences for the year. Keeping an accurate record of each staff member's annual leave days is essential to ensure that they are neither taking more than their entitlement nor being short-changed. It is possible to purchase commercially developed forms for use or you can design your own. Records must be kept for a minimum of six years.

The employer's duties are:

- to provide a written health and safety policy, if there are more than five members of staff and to ensure that each member of staff has access to a leaflet or poster entitled 'Health and Safety Law: What You Should Know'
- to operate a PAYE system. The employer must deduct and pay the appropriate amount of tax, employee's national insurance contributions and employer's national insurance contributions for each member of staff. There are hefty penalties if you fail to do so
- to operate a Statutory Sick Pay (SSP) scheme. After four days of sickness absence from work the employee is due a minimum statutory payment. This does not affect any contractual arrangements made with the employee for sick leave being unpaid. There is a formula for calculating the amount of SSP which can be claimed back from national insurance payments
- to operate a Statutory Maternity Pay (SMP) system with maternity leave arrangements for any pregnant employee. This applies to staff directly employed on temporary or short-term contracts as well as those employed on a more permanent basis. Guidance is available from your local Social Security office about staff entitlements and what employers are obliged to do. There is also advice on how to reclaim the amounts of SMP which you have paid out.

Keeping the employment relationship going

Once the staff team has been engaged you will be faced with another array of responsibilities and issues to deal with. Whilst it is important to fulfil your legal obligations, you also need to consider how you will act as an employer. Some basic ways of maintaining good employment relationships are listed here.

- Provide clear written information for staff about what is expected of them.
- Regularly talk with and listen to the staff.
- Respect everyone's individual skills and personal qualities.
- Deal even-handedly with all staff.
- Avoid personalising issues, gossiping, scapegoating and defaming individuals.
- Do not make commitments which cannot be met when the time comes.
- Do use your discretionary powers, but within an equitable framework.
- Plan and write down protocols and forms for each personnel function; then use them.
- Keep records and up-to-date staff files.
- Know the contents of the contracts and check them again before acting.
- Have a budget for ongoing legal advice.
- Keep abreast of case law, legislation and good practice.

Finally, it is vitally important to remember the context in which nursery staff are employed. If staff are expected to always be fair and caring towards children, then they must have confidence in their employer being fair and caring towards them.

Interviews as part of the employment framework

The interview format can be an effective management technique and some examples of different types of interviews are described below.

PROBATIONARY STAFF INTERVIEWS

Although traditional probationary status does not fit with current legislation, it is sensible to recognise that newer members of staff need some special attention. For example, time to settle in and guidance on the ethics and work routine are important. Interviews at, say, three-monthly intervals for the first year of employment (or promotion) can be mutually beneficial. One structure suitable for the interview is to refer to a document which focuses, one by one, on specific skills or areas of work. Employee's strengths deserve the same amount of attention as their weaknesses. Staff members should be encouraged to offer comments on what support would be appreciated. They should also be encouraged to identify any causes of unhappiness or disappointments with their jobs.

By maintaining a balanced, positive attitude, managers can help staff members to improve and also can help the nursery to identify actions to improve employment practices. Keeping a written record of the interviews is a good idea. Records become particularly significant if you eventually have to conclude that the member of staff is not capable (on skill or health grounds) of fulfilling the obligations of their contract. They also protect the nursery if claims of unfairness are made.

ANNUAL APPRAISAL INTERVIEWS

Many large companies have complex, sophisticated appraisal schemes which involve line management, goal setting, job promotion and even rates of pay. However, for the purposes of nursery management a simple system would be sufficient. The appraisal interview provides managers with the opportunity to express appreciation to staff for their efforts, to discuss any difficulties (but not disciplinary action), to share ideas and to explore aspirations. It should also be an opportunity to set some training targets and agree some improvements in performance. Whatever subjects are included, a completed appraisal form will help the manager and the member of staff to remember the dialogue and check on changes arising.

EXIT INTERVIEWS

Whenever a staff member gives notice that they are leaving, the manager should try to arrange a short, friendly interview. This exit interview offers the employer a setting in which to round off the employment relationship, express appreciation, wish staff well and to 'mend fences', if appropriate. If the employee is encouraged to express their thoughts, and if you listen acutely, it may be possible to identify strategies which need to be developed in order to retain staff. The exit interview is an opportunity for arranging details for the final pay cheque, P45, future references and return of keys or other property. It can also lay the foundations for an ongoing professional network with 'old bosses' and 'old employees' helping each other over time.

Conclusion

Employment has to be considered primarily in the context of its complex legal framework. However, it is also important to view all the staffing and human resources issues in the context of the nursery financial structures and childcare standards. Staff are key to the success of a nursery and are a resource to be carefully managed as well as nurtured.

Legal and financial advice are critical to managing the employment relationship. In addition to maintaining a link with specific advisers, nursery proprietors could benefit from a small library of guides to good practice and the law. The Arbitration Conciliation and Advisory Service (ACAS), the Institute of Personnel and Development (IPD, formerly IPM), the Commission for Racial Equality (CRE), the Equal Opportunities Commission (EOC) and the Health and Safety Executive (HSE), all produce specialist written materials which clarify the fine points of the relevant laws and codes of practice. The ACAS guides are particularly helpful in setting out practical advice on good practice. Commercially produced handbooks from Croners and Gees are reliable and comprehensive standard references, but they do function through a relatively expensive subscription system. The voluntary sector offers a range of literature dealing with aspects of employment related to childcare. The Code of Employment Practice published by the National Council of Voluntary Child Care Organisations is grounded in employment law, and is well organised for clarity.

CHECKLIST

Getting ready to recruit and employ staff
- Local authority requirements
- Staffing plan linked to the budget
- Job description for each post
- Person specification for each post
- Salary scales and benefits package for each post
- Policy and framework for equal opportunities
- Policy and framework for health and safety
- Application forms
- Details to send out about the nursery and each post
- Draft job advertisements

Interviewing arrangements
- Plan for short-listing
- Arrangements for venue and nursery visit
- Plan for conduct of interviews
- List of interview questions
- List of information to tell candidates
- Draft letter for applicants not short-listed for interview
- Draft letter to invite candidates to interview
- Draft letter to candidates who are unsuccessful at interview

Offering the job
- Information for a verbal offer
- Draft offer letter
- Draft conditions of service
- Draft letter to request references
- Draft health questionnaire
- Supply of forms for taking up police checks
- List of information required from staff
- Supply of record forms

12 HEALTH, SAFETY AND HYGIENE

> **What this chapter covers:**
> - Importance of health, safety and hygiene
> - Management of health and safety
> - Accident prevention
> - Preventing the spread of infection
> - Safe food handling
> - Safe nursery activities and outings
> - Dealing with accidents and providing First Aid
> - Fire protection

> 'Don't go into Mr McGregor's garden. Your father had an accident there;
> he was put into a pie by Mrs McGregor.'
>
> Beatrix Potter

In this chapter the key issues related to health, safety and hygiene are set out. It is an important area of responsibility for nursery management. Legal obligations to protect children, staff and visitors provide the most telling arguments for having good health, safety and hygiene practices. Legislation needs to be acknowledged and complied with and managing health and safety has to be a major preoccupation for everyone connected with the nursery.

Importance of health, safety and hygiene

As an employer you are responsible for the protection of your staff and are required to draw health and safety procedures to their attention both for their own benefit and that of the public. Children's interests are also protected by the main pieces of health and safety legislation as well as the standards identified in the Children Act Guidance. Local authority registration and inspection requirements sensibly place a significant emphasis on health and safety factors. A thorough understanding of the very wide range of issues and perspectives is essential in order to ensure that your nursery fulfils all its statutory obligations and that you can meet the somewhat more equivocal duty of care which is placed, by common law, on all adults involved in caring for children.

Children need to be able to explore and test out their environment as part of their general development. Consequently nurseries should be managed in a way which allows children the greatest possible freedom with the fewest possible risks. Adequate precautions are needed to ensure that any accidents or illnesses contracted in the nursery cause no lasting damage.

Staff need to be assured of safe and healthy working conditions so that they can pursue their responsibilities and have a satisfactory career. As an employer of more than five people you are required by law to have a written health and safety policy for the benefit of staff. You also have to pay particular regard to The Workplace Health Safety and Welfare Regulations Act 1992 which includes regulations about the work environment, ventilation, rest areas, eating facilities, housekeeping and maintenance. You have to look after your employees and provide them with statutory information either via a poster or the leaflet, entitled 'Health and Safety Law – What You Should Know', which is supplied by the Health and Safety Executive (HSE). There is also a duty to report to the HSE any accident to a member of staff which results in an absence of more than five working days.

Management of health and safety

It is prudent to take a managerial approach to dealing with health, safety and hygiene issues. Amongst the important aspects of your managerial obligations are responsibilities to ensure that there are adequate policies and procedures to set out standards and safe practices, communications networks to identify and bring risks to the attention of management and sufficient numbers of well-trained staff present at all times in the nursery. Managing the partnerships with parents is another highly important feature. They have a right to know what your policies and procedures are and they also need to understand their role and responsibilities with regard to all the health, safety and hygiene issues which affect the nursery.

FIVE STEPS TO MANAGEMENT

The HSE has usefully identified a managerial framework in their document 'Five Steps to Health and Safety Management'.

1. Set your policy. (Identify the issues by considering all the possible risks to staff and children, related to the daily routine and premises. Policies must be in writing including an indication of who is responsible for identifying and mitigating hazards.)
2. Organise your staff. (Decide and delegate – who is responsible for what, including provision of information and training.)
3. Plan and set standards. (Priorities must be appropriately identified, risks assessed and imminent dangers planned for.)
4. Measure your performance. (Keep accurate records which monitor the maintenance of your agreed standards. Investigate serious events as well as near misses.)
5. Learn from experience. Audit and review. (Identify gaps or inadequate standards. Also analyse trends and take action to improve things.)

HEALTH AND SAFETY REPORT		
Issues and events to be reported	Action points arising	Check against risk assessment
Accidents		
Fire protection		
Premises – interior and exterior		
Equipment – play and domestic		
Pets		
Staff health matters		
Child health matters		
Health education and training		
Major concerns, worries, questions		
General hygiene matters		
Other matters		

Report signed and submitted by: _____

Date: _____ Seen by Manager: _____

Company Director: _____

Example of a quarterly report of the health and safety officer

NAMED HEALTH AND SAFETY OFFICER

It may be suitable to designate one member of the nursery staff to take the lead on health and safety matters, with the nursery manager having ultimate responsibility. The health and safety officer will have to have opportunities to liaise with other staff, to raise discussion about relevant matters and to induct new team members or students into the appropriate procedures. The use of a set of forms, to assess and monitor risks, record events and report to management, will help to measure performance and to build on experience. Regularly scheduled management review meetings with the health and safety officer, and agreed action plans to follow up, should make the necessary links between the suggested five steps.

Accident prevention

Formalised risk management and reduction of as many hazards as possible are required by law under the Management of Health and Safety at Work Regulations 1992. These are intended to protect employees and any other persons likely to be affected by the conduct of a business. This includes children in the nursery and their parents. A suitably broad interpretation includes everything from how nappies are disposed of to the degree of slipperiness of a floor. It is recommended that the process of identifying hazards, evaluating the risks and recording the findings of your assessment, be carried out in a practical and uncomplicated way. However, risk assessment must be carried out and acted upon. Reduction of risks will require attention to a number of things such as premises design, provision of equipment, e.g. ladders and lockable cupboards, and regular checks on features such as high shelves and storage areas.

CHEMICALS

Hazardous chemical substances, which include the inevitable selection of cleaning supplies found in nurseries, should be looked at closely to ascertain their content, to have regard to the implications of manufacturers' warnings, to find out what remedies are listed on the labels and what action might be required to handle them or dispose of them safely. The significance of this information should be understood by all. Undoubtedly, qualified child carers will be conscientious in ensuring that such substances are locked away and that children are protected from the possibilities of touching, swallowing or inhaling them. However, cleaning staff, builders and students, etc. are likely to need to be reminded and should be supervised.

LIFTING AND CARRYING

Manual Handling Regulations also apply particularly to nurseries, though they will require some interpretation from what is anticipated in the standard HSE literature. There is a duty on the employer to assess the load, the environment and the worker. Training must be provided if necessary. Most training for nursery staff now incorporates advice on lifting techniques. Nevertheless it is wise to raise the level of awareness of staff members regularly and to encourage them to be careful when lifting and carrying children and to share the work of moving large items of equipment.

SAFETY DEVICES

General safety features such as internal gates, door locks, raised door handles, viewing panels in doors and safety closers on heavy doors should be incorporated into the design and equipping of the premises. A fair proportion of the initial equipment budget will be needed for safety equipment such as gym mats, safe storage, First Aid boxes, electric socket covers, etc.

SUPERVISING CHILDREN

A slightly different aspect of accident prevention to consider relates to the nursery routine. Provision has to be made to supervise children and to effectively have a continuous risk assessment approach with them. Fingers in doors, climbing on unstable surfaces, taking first steps in the midst of a boisterous game, all pose risks. Children's general behaviour and exuberance has to be channelled for their own safety and that of their friends. Behaviour which is out of control or children who are hidden away from general view are particular causes for concern and require action.

Preventing the spread of infection

Cross-infection is a high risk in a group situation. As a consequence, positive preventative action needs to be taken at a management level to mitigate the risks. This can include elements of premises design as well as maintenance. For example, the kitchen and other rooms where food is present must always be in a sound, hygienic condition in order to help to restrict the spread of infections and the possibility of food contamination. In addition to the kitchen, milk preparation area and other food rooms, there has to be a similar focus on the nappy change area, potty area, children's toilets and adult toilets.

The design of these areas should ensure the ease of cleaning and maintenance (so toilet cubicles should be large and any doors should be removable) and convenient siting of safe storage for cleaning materials, etc. Design and maintenance must be supported by particular planning and attention to policy on general practices, personal hygiene and cleaning. Routines for these areas (e.g. disinfecting potties after each use) and cleaning (e.g. washing the whole of the porcelain base of toilets) should be agreed in detail, preferably by the full staff team, written up and posted on appropriate notice boards as a reminder. It is impossible to stress strongly enough the importance of hand washing, hygienic

The budget will need to include adequate sums for cleaning materials

ways of dealing with vomit, accidents and nappy changing, and avoiding the use of germ-collecting dishcloths, tea towels, hand towels, etc.

The budget will need to include adequate sums for disposable items such as polythene gloves (used for protection against infections), cleaning cloths and nappy bags. Every sink and hand basin should be equipped with liquid soap and paper towels as well as (regularly disinfected) nail brushes.

EXCLUSIONS FOR INFECTIOUS AND NOTIFIABLE ILLNESSES

Your local Health Authority will have lists of the infectious illnesses for which children must be excluded from the nursery along with guidance on lengths of exclusions required. As part of the registration process this information should be made available to you. You will particularly need to share this information with parents, in part as reassurance about how their child is to be protected and in part so that they are aware of their obligation to notify the nursery of illnesses and to care for sick children at home. Most parents and visitors will expect the nursery to post a notice if there are children ill with measles or mumps, which could adversely affect pregnancy or fertility.

Notifiable diseases such as cholera, smallpox, tuberculosis, typhus, meningitis, diphtheria and food poisoning must be formally brought to the attention of the Environmental Health Department. All parents of children attending the nursery should also be notified, preferably in writing. Exclusion of the children and staff members affected will be required.

Safe food handling

The Food Safety Act 1990, The Food Premises Regulations 1991 and The Food Safety (Temperature Control) Regulations 1995 all apply to your nursery, which must be classified as a 'food business' because you provide food for the children. This means that you will need to complete a registration form provided by the Environmental Health Department and to comply with certain regulations and standards of kitchen design.

Hygiene regulations about the quality of the food, the way food is stored, the conditions under which meals are prepared, the personal hygiene habits of staff preparing food, and the condition and cleanliness of the kitchen will all have to be met. Procedures should be agreed with the cook and all staff who have access to food. Employing a trained cook can be a real advantage because they should understand the complexity of the issues and what standards are needed. Training in Safe Food Handling should be on offer locally and your registration is likely to require that your cook, and even the nursery manager, should attend a course.

Equipping the food preparation areas involves significant financial commitment. New refrigerators should ensure the necessary good door seals and even temperature. Ovens with sufficient volume and reliable temperature are essential to cook food thoroughly. Dishwashers cut down on germs which may be spread through the manual washing of dishes. A range of colour-coded chopping boards, storage containers and thermometers are required if possible contamination of cooked food or raw food is to be avoided. The provision of uniforms and head coverings for the cook and any kitchen assistants is accepted standard practice. As with other aspects of health and safety, skimping on equipment would be a recipe for problems.

BABY MILK AND FOOD PREPARATION

Special thought should be given to the preparation area and procedures for making up baby meals and bottles. All the usual design, equipment specifications, maintenance and hygiene practices should be carefully followed. There should also be very strict control over the process of making up bottles, so that staff know in detail about particular children's needs, types of formula milk, etc. and work in an environment where mistakes cannot happen (e.g. through interruptions). The youngest children are the most vulnerable to dehydration, tummy upsets and bacterial infections, which can too easily result from poor hygiene practices and inattention when mixing formulae milk. Consequently these children must have a very high degree of protection.

Safe nursery activities and outings

Obviously, all the equipment and toys being used by the children should comply with the relevant British Standard, be maintained in good condition and be safe for the age group using them. This means, for example, that loose screws should be tightened, sharp edges covered, items such as cots and high chairs regularly cleaned and disinfected and dressing up clothes laundered. Maintaining the necessary standard is an unrelenting activity which has to be built into the management structure and routine. The budget has to be adequate to meet the costs of maintenance or replacement.

Outings to libraries, local shops etc. should take place within the context of an established policy on safety which sets out standards such as the ratio of one adult to two children and the use of safety harnesses. Rarer outings to less familiar places, or activities off-site, such as swimming or dancing, must be planned in advance. Specific parental permission should be obtained and plans made for possible risks as well as contingencies for maintaining safety. Although this can be frightening to contemplate in the first instance, it should become so much a part of the management system that it enhances, rather than inhibits, outings.

Transportation for outings raises a number of health and safety concerns in addition to the insurance aspects. The Transport Act 1985 places particular requirements on organisations using minibuses or coaches. Regulations about vehicles carrying school age children (3–16) are effective from 1997. Whether you decide to buy your own minibus or hire transport as you need it, you should become familiar with the requirements. Appropriate seat belts must be fitted, each child should occupy one seat and not be crowded in, drivers must be over 21 with a current PSV driving licence, a fire extinguisher and First Aid kit should be on board and doors must comply with regulations for locking and opening.

Dealing with accidents and providing First Aid

From the day the nursery first opens you must have in place all the resources, as well as a appropriate policies and procedures, for dealing with accidents, however minor. The relevant information has to be clearly communicated and understood by all staff. Parents also need to know and have a right to written information about accident and First Aid practices.

ESSENTIAL POINTS

It is recommended that the policies and practices include the following as essential points.

- Children need to be comforted, calmed and not exposed to possible panic by staff.
- One member of staff should take responsibility for each injured child.
- First Aid must be administered and the need for a trip to hospital assessed.
- The response to an emergency must be quick and err on the side of caution.
- Child records indicating the details of the child's GP, allergies, parents' telephone numbers etc., should be taken to the hospital if hospital attention is required.

NURSERY ACCIDENT REPORT

Please complete a separate form for each person injured, even if in the same accident

Particulars of injured person
1. Name: _____
2. Designation (e.g. child, staff member, parent, visitor): _____
3. Normal hours of attendance/work at nursery on day of accident: _____

Particulars of accident as reported
1. Date of accident: _____ 2. Time of accident: _____
3. Place where the accident happened: _____
_____
4. Witnesses: _____
5. Description of the accident (indicate – how it happened, who was involved, what activity or work was being performed):
_____
_____
6. Description of injuries observed (state whether on left or right, etc.):
_____
_____
7. Treatment given, when, where and by whom:
_____
_____
8. Staff on duty in the area and description of their activities, at the time of the accident: _____
_____
9. Time and transport used etc. when the injured person left the nursery:
_____
10. Any additional information: _____
_____

Particulars of reporting of accident
1. If the accident was not reported by the injured person, who reported it? When? How? _____
_____
2. Any other information: _____
_____

REQUIRED SIGNATURES:
Report completed by: _____ Date: _____
Report seen by Manager:_____ Date: _____
Report seen by Company Director: _____ Date: _____
Report seen by parent/injured person: _____ Date: _____
Comments: _____
_____

Example of a nursery accident report

- Some staff must immediately take responsibility for supervision of the other children.
- Adults and children who witness an accident need comfort and attention to cope with shock.
- Parents need to be contacted about serious accidents as they happen.
- Parents need to be told at the end of the day about any accident, even a minor bump.
- A full investigation and written report of the accident should be immediately undertaken.

All the same procedures should apply if a member of staff has an accident or takes sick at work. It really is an employer's responsibility to see that they reach home or hospital safely even if it necessitates sending another member of staff with them.

HOSPITAL ATTENTION

Young babies, children with chronic conditions, allergies or other special needs may require First Aid and/or hospital treatment if they become ill at nursery. It is important that staff have a clear understanding of what immediate steps to take and that there is an agreed procedure which has been worked out with the parents. Parents will probably have useful expertise to share with nursery staff and this should be tapped for the benefit of the children.

PREVENTING COT DEATH

Staff in nurseries which provide for young babies have to be vigilant in following the procedures which reduce the likelihood of cot death. Specific information is available from the Foundation for the Study of Infant Deaths. The type of cot bedding, a constant room temperature (24 °C or 75 °F), the position of the baby when put down to sleep and the location of sleep areas follow as a matter of best practice. Staff also need to have a thorough understanding of the general vulnerabilities of babies and the rapidity with which they can become seriously ill. Good observation and First Aid skills are critical.

FIRST AID TRAINING

First Aid training is a must. Your nursery registration and annual inspections will probably require proof of the employment of two qualified First Aiders. Although most nursery nurses do receive basic First Aid training, the certificated courses (usually three full days) run by organisations such as St. John's Ambulance and the Red Cross are the ones most likely to be recognised for registration. Certificates are valid for a specified period of time and refresher training and examination must be undertaken before the expiry date if renewal is to be obtained. The provision and maintenance of several First Aid boxes in appropriate locations (including the kitchen and staff room) is required.

Fire protection

The Fire Services Act 1970 and the Fire Precautions Act 1971 regulate means of escape, conditions of premises, provision of fire appliances and smoke detectors, etc. During the premises design and registration processes, the nursery will be inspected and you will be advised about your fundamental obligations. Additional information about annual maintenance of fire appliances and training in their use should be followed; so should recommendations made for the best practice in fire safety arrangements.

FIRE PRACTICE

Regular fire practices will need to be held. They should be used as an opportunity for every adult to understand what is required of them, to give children the experience of fire practices and to assess the viability of evacuation procedures, including assembly points and the time taken. Particular thought will need to be given to how best to get children safely from the nursery to the assembly point and how to evacuate small babies and children with special needs. The register, containing up-to-date telephone numbers for parents, should always be taken out to the assembly point so that all children can be accounted for and parents contacted if necessary. It may be useful to have a pre-packed bag with nappies, water, blankets etc. for the comfort of babies. Finally, it should not be forgotten that all adults should be accounted for as well.

Conclusion

Health, safety and hygiene necessarily have a high priority in nursery provision because of the importance of protecting the children and the staff team. The legislative framework, policies to be followed and standards to be maintained have to be shared and understood by all staff and parents. Many of the simplest measures, such as risk assessment, regular hand washing and thoroughly cleaning kitchen work surfaces, can be of the greatest benefit in protecting everyone's health.

Primary sources of guidance include the local authority registration requirements, the local fire service and the Health and Safety Executive. The voluntary sector, especially the Child Accident Prevention Trust, have a number of cogent publications. Commercial suppliers of fire and safety equipment can also offer helpful technical information.

CHECKLIST

Policies and procedures
- Health and safety
- Information for staff and parents
- Role of health and safety officer

CHECKLIST continued

- Students and visitors
- Premises risk assessment
- Activities risk assessment
- Safe outings
- Safe transportation
- Hazardous substances
- Lifting and carrying
- Accident prevention
- Dealing with accidents
- Children with special health needs
- Control of infections
- Exclusions for infectious illnesses
- Fire practices
- Food preparation and hygiene standards
- Food storage
- Hygiene routines for each room in the nursery
- Premises cleaning routine

Equipment and materials
- First Aid boxes
- Fire appliances
- Smoke detectors and alarms
- Signs to mark fire routes
- Gates and doors to control exit and entry
- Locks and closers on doors and gates
- Safety mats and soft surfaces for active play
- Electric socket covers and cable tacks
- Refrigerator and freezer thermometers
- Room thermometers
- Disposable gloves and cleaning cloths
- Safe storage for cleaning materials etc.
- Paper towels, liquid soap and nail brushes

13 *MARKETING*

Life is like a bicycle. You don't fall off unless you stop pedalling.

Claude Pepper

This chapter is about making sure parents have information about your nursery. We suggest where to advertise or post information about your nursery in order to make information available to as many people as possible cost-effectively. You will need to make sure you have material ready for your marketing, and to follow up enquiries – we suggest what material you should prepare. Finally we look at ways in which you can monitor the effectiveness of your advertising, so that you can make sure you are spending your advertising budget in the best way, and giving your nursery maximum coverage.

Where to advertise

Marketing and attracting parents to your nursery will take considerable time in the first year of operation, and it is easy to underestimate the time and effort involved. It is sensible to prepare a marketing plan before you open your nursery, so that you know exactly where you plan to advertise your nursery, what materials you will need and when you will advertise. In order to do this you will need to examine the various ways of advertising and marketing, the practicalities and the costs involved.

During your market research you will have gathered information which will help you decide where to advertise your nursery. It is worth deciding what you are endeavouring to achieve through your advertising. Generally for a nursery this will be to inform parents living or working locally of your nursery and the service you offer. You will therefore need to find out where parents go for information about childcare.

WATCH POINT

Parents often hear about nurseries through word of mouth, but until you become well established locally, you will need to work hard at ensuring parents know about your nursery rather than simply relying on this method.

Parents often hear about nurseries through word of mouth

You should also advertise widely to ensure that, from an equal opportunities perspective, you are offering access to all community groups – not excluding some because they are not part of the right networks or do not happen to look in the places in which you advertise. You should advertise in places accessible to all the community, and it is good practice to advertise in minority papers.

Typically it is best to consider a mix of the following for regular advertising.

LOCAL PAPERS

The quality of local papers varies, and in some places it is debatable whether parents would look in a local paper for a good nursery. Nevertheless, advertising your nursery in a local paper is a good way of maintaining local awareness, and ensuring that information about your nursery is available to as many sections of the local community as possible.

YELLOW PAGES

Many parents consult the local Yellow Pages directory when looking for a nursery. Some ring all of the nurseries listed to obtain details. You should ensure that you obtain your free listing in your local directory. In some areas it is also worth paying for an entry in a neighbouring directory (e.g. in London where your catchment area crosses boundaries between the various Yellow Pages directories covering the London area.)

LOCAL AUTHORITY LIST OF NURSERIES

All local authorities have lists of nurseries, sometimes incorporated in an Under-eights Guide. This is a valuable reference for parents looking for childcare, and you should make sure that your nursery is listed, with the correct details.

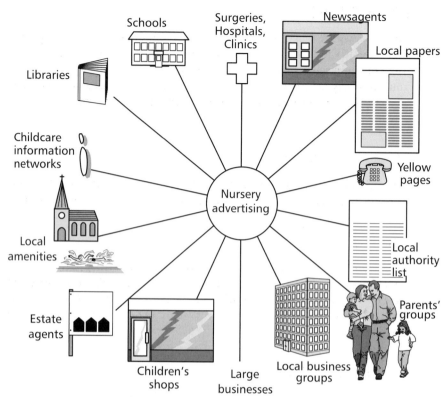

Making information available about your nursery

NEWSLETTERS DISTRIBUTED BY LOCAL PARENTS' GROUPS

There are usually a number of local networks and groups for parents, and many have newsletters which are distributed to their members. The charges for advertising are generally modest, so this is a very cost-effective method of highly targeted advertising. Organisations to contact include the National Childbirth Trust and Parents at Work.

NEWSLETTERS DISTRIBUTED THROUGH LOCAL BUSINESS GROUPS

This can be a good way of advertising your nursery to local employers as well as to working parents. Organisations such as the Chamber of Commerce usually have newsletters. There may also be a business forum arranged by the local authority.

LOCAL SHOPS

Children's clothes shops, toy shops, book shops and baby equipment shops, which parents visit regularly, often have noticeboards on which you can advertise. Some charge a small weekly fee, while others ask for a donation to charity. You could pay an amount in advance, say for six months, so that you know your advert will remain there – but it is worth sending a new copy every few months as the adverts tend to need refreshing.

LOCAL AMENITIES

Swimming pools, community centres, church halls and other local amenities usually have noticeboards, and are pleased to have information about local services.

LIBRARIES

Local residents use their library as a reference point, and most libraries have noticeboards on which you will be able to advertise. You can either take your advert to the library, or send it with a note to the librarian. It is worth doing this regularly (say quarterly) as the library staff tend to tidy up their noticeboards every so often.

HEALTH FACILITIES

Doctors' surgeries, health centres, ante-natal clinics and dentists' surgeries are all used regularly by parents, and most of these facilities have noticeboards or information racks on which you can place adverts. You could leave a batch of leaflets so that parents can take one away with them. You might also leave some leaflets with health visitors, practice nurses or mid-wives to pass on to patients who they know are looking for childcare. Health visitors are an excellent source of referrals, especially if you are offering baby places.

LOCAL SCHOOLS

It is worth making contact with local schools, especially those to which the children in your nursery will progress. Teachers are often asked if they know of good local nurseries, and the schools may have parents' noticeboards on which you could display leaflets for your nursery.

LOCAL NEWSAGENTS

Many local newsagents or corner shops show adverts in their shop windows. This can be a good, cost-effective way of informing parents about your service. However, the adverts need refreshing regularly.

ESTATE AGENTS

Families moving into the area are quite likely to ask an estate agent about child-care facilities. Some agents will display literature in their offices, or keep information on file for families who make enquiries about local childcare. Others have maps or leaflets on which local businesses can advertise. It is also worth making contact with relocation agents who make arrangements for staff of large companies when they are relocated. They often have the task of seeking out schools and childcare.

LARGE EMPLOYERS

If you have large employers in your area, it is worth approaching them through their personnel departments to find out if they are interested in purchasing nursery places for their employees. Some large companies have information networks for their staff in which information about your nursery could be included.

CHILDCARE INFORMATION NETWORKS

These are important reference points for parents seeking information on childcare and children's services generally. If you have such a network in your area it will be important to make sure that your nursery is listed with the service.

LEAFLETING

In addition to regular advertising, you might also consider leafleting, especially when you first open your nursery. However, this is time consuming, and it is difficult to target solely at parents. Organisations such as the Royal Mail do offer a service, but they can only leaflet by postcode. This makes it a rather random, widespread and costly exercise. However, if you have a relatively tight catchment area, this may be worth considering.

Marketing material

The material you will need will depend on where you choose to advertise. If you are using a mix of the above methods of advertising, you will need to prepare the following:

- a leaflet to place on noticeboards or to use for leaflet distribution
- an advert to place in newspapers or newsletters
- a nursery prospectus to send to parents who contact you
- other information you may wish to give to parents, e.g. a statement of your childcare policy, an example of an activity programme or an example of a typical nursery day.

You must ensure that your adverts and literature are neither sexist nor racist, either overtly or by implication.

You may decide to pay for some design assistance in preparing your marketing material, although this can be expensive (grants are sometimes available from the local authority). Alternatively you could prepare something simple yourself and reproduce it using the facilities of a local photocopy shop. They will be able to help you choose paper colour and quality, and advise you on the options for typesetting, printing, photocopying or colour copying.

You will need to weigh up the need for:

■ a good, strong, appropriate image
■ a consistent image across all your material
■ good quality production
■ flexibility – you may wish to change the wording on your leaflets or in your prospectus over time
■ material which fits your budget.

Collecting prospectuses or information leaflets from other local nurseries or schools may give you some ideas.

Generally newspapers will typeset your adverts free of charge. However, the production team will not necessarily follow your house style or develop a layout with a good visual impact without very precise instructions. You will need to make sure you see a copy of the advert before it goes to press to avoid disappointment. When placing adverts with newspapers you should always discuss a discount, especially if you plan to advertise regularly.

You might also like to obtain some coverage in local newspapers or magazines. To do this you will need to prepare a press release focusing on a story. For example, you might have an opening party inviting a local dignitary, or your nursery might be the first to open in your area, or the first to offer baby facilities.

You will need to make sure that you have the necessary material and information to take parents through to registering their child at the nursery. This might include:

■ a printed letterhead on which to prepare any correspondence with prospective parents
■ details of how to contact the nursery
■ details of how to find the nursery
■ a list of the nursery fees
■ a standard application form
■ a standard form of letter to offer parents a place for their child
■ standard terms and conditions for using the nursery (these could be included in the prospectus)
■ a statement of how you will allocate places and deal with any waiting lists.

Monitoring effectiveness

It is important to monitor the effectiveness of your marketing programme. This will help you make sure that you are disseminating information as widely as possible and in places where parents will find it. It will also help you decide whether or not you are spending your publicity budget well. Without this you might find

Make sure you have the necessary material and information for parents

yourself in the position of one Chief Executive of a large company 'I know that 50% of my advertising is wasted. The trouble is, I don't know which 50%'.

Monitoring is carried out most effectively by asking parents how they heard about the nursery. You can ask them this when they first contact the nursery – if you keep a pad of contact sheets by the telephone the nursery staff will be able to jot down the details. You can also ask parents on the enrolment form when they enrol their child.

Through monitoring at these two levels you will be able to look at where parents tend to hear about your nursery, and to identify where parents who actually enrol their children find out about the nursery. For example, you may find that you have a lot of enquiries in response to adverts in the local paper, but that none of these parents go on to enrol their children.

This information will also enable you to begin to look at 'conversion rates'. On average what percentage of people contacting the nursery for information actually enrol their child? This will enable you to gauge likely enrolments – if your conversion rate is one in ten, and you are having on average five families per week contacting the nursery, then you can expect only around two enrolments per month.

Conclusion

Effective marketing is vital in the early days, but is also just as important as your nursery becomes established. You will always have children moving on, and need to ensure that you sustain awareness within the local community of the service you offer.

CHECKLIST

Preparing a marketing plan
- Effectiveness and cost of adverts
- Targeted leaflet distribution and cost
- Other types of marketing and costs
- Lead time for each
- Final plan with dates and costs

Implementing a marketing plan
- Adverts
- Leaflets
- Prospectus
- Booked adverts
- Yellow Pages
- Local authority list
- Local group contacts
- Mailing – libraries, health visitors, clinics
- Local employers
- Local children's facilities
- Local schools
- Local shops
- Estate agents
- Press releases

Monitoring marketing effectiveness
- Record of how parents hear about the nursery
- Regular review of other advertising mechanisms
- Adjustments to plan
- Statistics on number of enquiries and percentage enrolment

14 FINANCIAL MANAGEMENT

> **What this chapter covers:**
> - **The importance of financial management**
> - **Choosing a financial structure**
> - **Accounting records**
> - **Financial monitoring and planning**
> - **PAYE records**
> - **Other financial matters**

Look after the pennies and the pounds will look after themselves.

English proverb

In this chapter we look at the various financial structures which are appropriate for a nursery. We suggest how to set about keeping accounting records, and detail the main records you will need to keep. Paying staff is an important regular financial matter, for which you have particular legal obligations. There are also several sundry financial matters which deserve attention.

The importance of financial management

When you open your nursery there will be essentially two main reasons why your venture may not succeed. The first is that you may not provide a sufficiently high standard of childcare, so that parents are reluctant to use your nursery or, at the very worst, you lose your registration. The second is that you run out of money. Strong financial management is therefore an essential element of the management of your nursery.

You may not have a detailed understanding of book-keeping and accountancy, and may decide to delegate much of this to your accountant, but it is important that you develop a good understanding of the financial dynamics of your nursery, and monitor its progress. Also, in the early years you may not be able to afford to pay an accountant for a full service. It may be better to take on the basic book-keeping yourself, and retain your accountancy budget to pay your accountant for advice on more complex matters.

Should you decide to undertake your own book-keeping, you may choose to refer to a detailed textbook on book-keeping and accounting, or your accountant may be able to help get you started. Alternatively, your local TEC may be a good source of advice or may run short courses in book-keeping for those setting up their own business. In any event, you should engage an accountant to help you set up your business, and to complete all the necessary formalities on an ongoing basis. A good accountant should also be an excellent source of advice to help you manage your nursery into a healthy financial position.

Choosing a financial structure

You will need to set up an appropriate financial structure for your nursery. Your accountant will be able to explain in detail the differences between the various options open to you, and the implications of each. Generally there are three options.

A COMPANY LIMITED BY SHARES

This limits your liability to the amount of share capital you put into the business, although you may be asked as a director to guarantee personally certain liabilities such as a bank loan, overdraft, mortgage or rent payments. Under this structure, which you can also use if you set up your nursery with a business partner, you would have to deduct PAYE and National Insurance contributions (NICs) from any income you take out of the business, and pay employer's National Insurance contributions on your income. The company will also be liable to corporation tax on its profits.

SOLE TRADER

Operating as a sole trader can have tax advantages as you will probably fall within Schedule D (self-employed status) for income tax purposes. However, you will have unlimited personal liability with respect to the business.

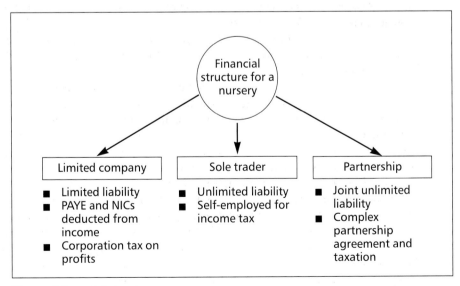

Types of financial structure

PARTNERSHIP

You can set up a partnership if you are going into business with another person. This involves setting up a partnership agreement, which can be complicated. The taxation of partnerships is also complex, and you would certainly need to take advice from your accountant. Under a partnership arrangement you and your partner would have joint personal unlimited liability for the partnership's debts.

Your accountant will be able to help you make the necessary arrangements to set up whichever structure you choose, and to complete the necessary formalities with regard to income tax, PAYE and VAT.

Accounting records

It is essential to maintain books of account for your business. You will need to do this in order to:

- keep track of your financial position
- maintain certain records for PAYE/NICs, income tax and VAT (if relevant – see below), and you are required by law to make these records available to the relevant inspectors if requested
- prepare an annual set of accounts for submission to HM Inspector of Taxes
- file your accounts each year at Companies House (if you are set up as a limited company).

There are strict deadlines for filing accounts, and potentially hefty fines if you do not comply with these deadlines. You should liaise closely with your accountant who will help you ensure that you comply.

You will need to decide how much of the book-keeping to do yourself, and how much to delegate to your accountant. This is something you should discuss with your accountant – he or she may be able to help you set up your books of account and provide you with sufficient tuition to get you going. Alternatively, you may find it easier to ask your accountant to do everything, but the books would need to be updated on a monthly basis so that you can monitor your financial position regularly, and you would need to have sufficient money available to pay an accountant to do this.

You may find general texts on book-keeping helpful to get you started. The following ideas will help you interpret general accounting principles in the context of a nursery.

ACCOUNT HEADINGS

First you will have to decide what account headings you will need to use, and give each one a number. The account headings you use should be grouped into four categories.

You will need to decide what account headings to use

Assets

These are items you purchase which are durable and will last some period of time, and anything else you own which has value, e.g. cash in the bank or money people owe you. For a nursery the asset headings would include:

- property
- furniture and large items of equipment
- toys, games, books etc.
- cash at bank
- petty cash
- fees due from parents
- milk grant due.

Liabilities

These are sums of money you owe to third parties, or expenditure you have incurred but for which you have not yet received an invoice (known as accruals). Typically these would include:

- bank loans or overdrafts
- loans from directors/proprietor
- PAYE/NICs deducted, but not yet paid
- trade creditors
- deposits paid to you by parents
- fees paid in advance.

Income

The headings in this category should cover all the categories of income you receive. This may simply be nursery fees, but you may also receive grants, or generate income from the sale of other products such as photographs or T-shirts.

Expenditure

You will need headings for every type of expenditure you incur. You may find it helpful to group them as follows:

- staff costs
- establishment costs
- nursery expenses
- legal, professional and finance
- central expenses.

PRIMARY RECORDS

You should develop your own form of record keeping, but you will find you need to maintain the following eight types of primary records in order to prepare your accounts.

Cash book

This is a key record of account, and records all the money you receive through your bank account, and all payments made from the bank account. If you have more than one bank account you will need to maintain more than one cash book. It is usually best to itemise receipts and payments under various account headings, which will help you analyse your payments and receipts when you prepare the journal entries for your month end accounts.

Bank statements

You should keep all of your bank statements. These are an essential records of your business transactions.

Petty cash book

This is your record of cash expenditure by the nursery staff. Details of these records are provided in the Chapter 5. You should retain all the invoices and receipts with the petty cash records.

Register of nursery fees with invoices

You will need to maintain a register or list of all the fees due from parents each month, taking account of children who have joined or left, any changes due to children moving up to the next age group, and any extra days children attend the nursery. You will need this listing in order to check that all fees due are paid.

List of all invoices received

This list should include details of when each invoice was paid. This is to keep track of what money you owe and to whom. At the end of each month you will need to analyse the expenditure under the appropriate account headings in order to prepare the journal entries for the accounts.

Expense records
Personal expense records for staff and directors are used to record any expenses paid for personally by your staff or you, which are then reimbursed by the business.

Payroll records
Full details of the payroll records you must maintain are provided later in this chapter.

Register of deposits paid by parents
It is very important that you maintain this record accurately as it is your main record of money parents have paid to you which you will have to repay when their child leaves the nursery. You should keep a record of the amount paid on behalf of each child.

ACCOUNTING ENTRIES

At the end of each month you will need to prepare the accounting entries from your primary records to input into your accounts package or spreadsheet using a double entry (debit and credit) book-keeping system. Your accounting system may be manual (very time consuming) or on a computer spreadsheet which you develop yourself, or on a commercially available computer package.

From your spreadsheet or accounts package you should produce a Trial Balance, which is a listing of the balances on each account. You should prepare various checks on this to verify that it is correct, then make any necessary adjustments (see next section). You should then group your account headings to produce a balance sheet and profit and loss account for the month.

CHECKS AND BALANCES

It is important to set up a series of checks and controls to verify the accuracy of your accounting records and controls. Typically these should include the following.

Casting
Casting and cross-casting all schedules to check that you have added them up correctly both vertically and horizontally is an important check.

Bank reconciliation
This is a standard accounting control, and involves agreeing the balance in your cash book at the end of the month with the balance as shown on your bank statement. In order to do this you will need to identify any receipts or payments recorded in your cash book which have not yet cleared through the bank

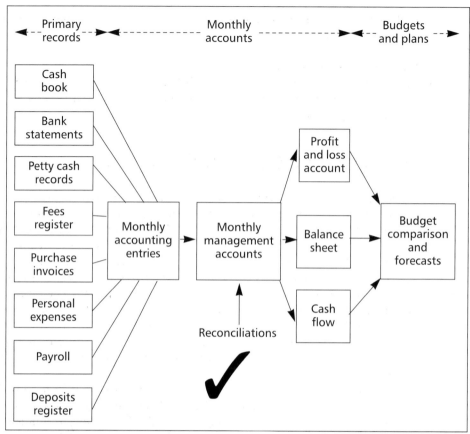

Keeping and using accounting records

account, and any items recorded on the bank statement which you have not recorded in your cash book.

Petty cash reconciliation
You should check the balance on the petty cash account according to your trial balance with the cash recorded as counted by your nursery staff at the end of the month.

Creditors reconciliation
You should add up all the outstanding invoices which you have not paid at the end of the month, and agree this to the trade creditors balance on your trial balance. Any difference would indicate that you have not recorded all your expenditure or all of your payments to creditors.

Fees reconciliation
This is to agree the total fees on your register of fees, net of any adjustments, to the fees recorded in your accounts. You should also agree the balance on your

trial balance for fees due and fees paid in advance to your listing of individual amounts by child.

PAYE/NICs reconciliation

The balance on this account in your trial balance should be the previous month's PAYE and NICs due, plus any amounts you have underpaid in previous months (or less any overpayment you have made).

Financial monitoring and planning

Having prepared your accounts (or having had them prepared for you), you should spend some time reviewing your financial position, and planning ahead.

The first step in this monitoring process is to look at the profit and loss for the month, and compare it with your budget item by item. Are there any major differences? What is the reason for each of these differences? Did you underbudget or did you overspend? Is there anything you can do to avoid this in future months? Or are the differences simply due to the timing of expenditure? For example, perhaps you budgeted for a purchase of more toys and games this month, but that order is not going through until next month, in which case you must still plan for that expenditure. You should be looking for differences which will need to be controlled if the financial stability of the nursery is not to be jeopardised.

You should then prepare a rolling three- or six-month profit and loss forecast, using your known enrolments. This will help you to identify any expected change in your financial position, and to consider what action you might take. Perhaps you will need to step up your marketing. Or perhaps your income is about to drop because of a group of babies is moving up to the next age group, in which case you should advertise your vacancies for baby places. Or is your staff cover overly generous given your enrolment pattern? Or are you over-reliant on temporary staff – could you actually reduce your costs by taking on permanent staff (which would in any case be better from the children's perspective)?

The next step is to convert this forecast into a three- or six-month rolling cash flow forecast, so that you can monitor whether or not you will have sufficient cash to pay your bills. If the forecast shows that you will not, you should speak to your bank immediately – trading while insolvent is a serious matter. Alternatively, you may be generating cash surpluses. Could you use these more effectively by opening a deposit account? Or perhaps now is the time to plan those refurbishments you have wanted to carry out for some time?

It is also worth looking at some key ratios to help you understand your financial structure, and whether there is anything you can sensibly alter to improve your financial position. You should expect these ratios to be broadly in line with the same ratios calculated from your cost structure for a full nursery. If they are out of line you should try to understand why, and decide whether there is any action you need to consider taking (with reference of course to operational con-

The rolling cash flow forecast

siderations – you must not prejudice the level and standard of care you are providing). Typically these ratios are:

- number of staff : enrolments
- total staff costs : fees
- temporary staff costs : salaries plus NIC
- food costs per child
- hygiene costs per child
- outings and activities costs per child
- administration : total costs.

Clearly this monitoring process will need to link in with your review of operations; you cannot manage the finances in isolation. You need to review your budgets and forecast in the light of what is actually going on in the nursery, balancing this with the need for careful financial control and strict financial discipline.

As part of your forecasting process it is well worth reviewing your capital and maintenance budget on a periodic basis, and developing a programme of maintenance and improvement for the nursery. This way you will be able to plan your capital expenditure to spend your money wisely as and when it is available, prioritising expenditure to the greatest advantage for the nursery.

PAYE records

You will be required by law to operate a PAYE system, including Statutory Sick Pay, for employees. This involves deducting tax and national insurance from your employees' pay, and paying this monthly to HM Collector of Taxes. You will also have to pay employer's national insurance contributions. Further, your employees are entitled by law to a payslip detailing their gross pay, all deductions and their net pay.

Your accountant will help you register with the appropriate tax office which will give you a reference number and send you their employer's starter pack. This has details of what records to keep, what to do each month, what to do if someone joins or leaves, how to make the necessary calculations and what to do at the end of the year. The pack will include the tax and national insurance tables you will need in order to calculate the deductions and payments.

If you do not wish to administer the payroll yourself, there are companies which provide a payroll service for small businesses (your accountant should be able to suggest a name or may also offer this service), but the ultimate responsibility for paying staff and deducting tax and national insurance remains yours.

The ultimate responsibility for paying staff is yours

There are a few things worth considering when setting up your payroll system:

- how frequently will you pay staff? Monthly will be the most efficient and advantageous for you, but will your staff be used to being paid monthly? Will you make any exceptions, e.g. for a few months when a new person joins? If you do, will your system be able to cope?
- what payment method will you use? Cash is inadvisable for security reasons, and is an expensive way of making payments – bank charges are very high for handling cash. Payment by cheque is acceptable, although this means that staff have to go to their banks to pay in their cheques, which is unlikely to be easy within the nursery day. Payment direct to an employee's bank account is a good method and is easy to set up. It is simple for you, convenient for staff and a low-cost method of payment. Your bank will be able to help you set this up
- on which day of the month will you pay staff? From a cash flow point of view the end of the month is ideal, but you will need to balance this with staff needs and preferences. It is sensible to set out a schedule at the beginning of

the year stating the dates on which staff will be paid, taking account of weekends or bank holidays, and to distribute this to your staff. You will need to remember that this is the day on which your employees will expect their money to arrive in their bank account, so you should find out from your bank how many days you should allow for the payment to reach individual accounts

■ will you maintain manual or computer records, or a mixture of both? The Inland Revenue deduction cards are easy to use manually, but it may be sensible to construct other records, such as payslips and summary schedules, on a computer spreadsheet. Larger companies input the tax and national insurance tables onto a computer which then carries out all the necessary calculations, but this could not possibly be justified for one nursery

■ you might want to enter your payroll payment dates and the dates for paying the tax and national insurance (19th of the following month) into your diary system – in the day-to-day running of the nursery it is very easy to forget to do the payroll, but this is one of the fastest ways to disenchant your staff!

Other financial matters

NURSERY EDUCATION GRANT

Four year olds attending your nursery may be eligible to receive a Nursery Education Grant. The grant, funded by the DfEE, is paid to you by the local authority, and must be refunded to parents or offset against their fees. Your local authority Early Years Department should be able to provide you with information about how to receive the grant. You will need to be registered under the DfEE scheme, and comply with the conditions and requirements of the grant. These include agreeing to be part of your local authority Early Years Partnership, working towards a specified set of desirable outcomes, meeting certain conditions with regard to staffing, special educational needs and insurance, maintaining appropriate administrative and financial records and agreeing to be inspected by OFSTED and the National Audit Office. A guide for providers claiming the nursery education grant is available from the DfEE.

MILK GRANT

You will be able to claim a grant from the Health Department towards milk for the children. Your local authority registration officer will tell you how and where to apply. You have to complete an initial registration form, and then claim the grant every four months in arrears. You will need to provide receipts for your purchases of milk.

VAT

If your nursery is registered under The Children Act, your service should be exempt from VAT. Consequently you should not have to register for VAT and should not have to charge VAT on nursery fees, but neither will you be able to reclaim any VAT on your purchases, e.g. equipment, agency fees or building work. You should ask your accountant to confirm this with HM Customs & Excise. Some nurseries opt for voluntary registration if they have other sources of income which are subject to VAT. It is then possible to reclaim some VAT under the partial exemption scheme. Advice on this is best obtained from your accountant or from a firm which specialises in recovering VAT. You will also have to weigh up the benefits of recovering a small amount of VAT against the time it will take to prepare the VAT return each quarter.

INSURANCE

You must maintain an up-to-date insurance policy at all times. As a minimum this should cover your premises and their contents, and public and employer's liability insurance. You might also consider additional cover such as the loss of revenue, legal fees or sickness and accident cover for your staff. Insurance policies specially designed for nurseries are available, and your insurance broker should be able to help you identify the best one for you.

Conclusion

With a thorough approach to financial management you should have sufficient information on a timely basis to understand the financial dynamics of your nursery, to identify any potential problems or difficulties as early as possible and to decide what action to take. This discipline will be especially important to you during the first few years of operation.

CHECKLIST

Starting out
- Engage an accountant
- Decide on a financial structure
- Complete the formalities
- Notify the tax office
- Confirm the VAT position

Setting up accounting records
- Cash book
- Bank statements
- Petty cash records
- Fees register and invoices
- List of creditors and invoices
- Expense records
- Payroll records
- Register of deposits

CHECKLIST continued

Checks and balances
- Castings
- Bank reconciliation
- Petty cash reconciliation
- Creditors reconciliation
- Fees reconciliation
- PAYE reconciliation

Monitoring and planning
- Comparison with budget
- Variance investigation
- Profit forecast
- Cash flow forecast
- Key ratios

Setting up the payroll
- Method of payment
- Frequency of payment
- Payment dates
- Manual or computer?
- Employers' starter pack from tax office
- Deduction worksheets and payment records
- Payslips
- Information for employees

Nursery Education Grant
- Initial registration
- Compliance with conditions

Milk grant
- Initial registration
- Claim every four months

VAT
- Exempt?
- Voluntary registration?

Insurance
- Premises and contents
- Public liability
- Employer's liability
- Other

15 CUSTOMER SERVICE AND PARENTAL INVOLVEMENT

> **What this chapter covers:**
> ■ Customer service in a nursery context
> ■ Communication with parents
> ■ Complaints, accidents and other difficult issues

The customer is always right.

Old English saying

This chapter is about communicating with parents. Throughout the 1990s businesses have focused on customer service as a route to gaining and retaining customers. In this chapter we explore some of these ideas, and explain how they can work in a nursery context where there are particular statutory responsibilities towards the child. We offer suggestions for fostering good relations with parents through effective communication, and discuss how to handle complaints and other difficult issues in a positive way.

Customer service in a nursery context

THINKING ABOUT YOUR CUSTOMERS

Strictly speaking your customers are the children attending your nursery. They have to be the main focus of your operation, and everything which happens in your nursery should be in the best interests of these children.

Nevertheless your service is purchased by parents on behalf of their children, and in this sense they are also your customers. They exercise choice on behalf of their children, and are guided by the happiness and well-being of their children.

Customer service has become the watchword of the 1990s. Most businesses, whether large or small, see customer retention as a key element of their strategy, and are concentrating on improving customer service. As customer service standards have improved across all business sectors and within the public sector, people have come to expect higher levels of customer service and responsiveness from all businesses and organisations with whom they have contact.

Consequently the parents using your nursery will have expectations which are set by their interactions with other businesses, e.g. mail order services, retailers and utilities, many of which have invested heavily to improve their service levels and to orientate their services to the customer. In relation to their children, parents will also have a set of expectations about how their children will be cared for.

Although parents will be concerned primarily that their child is well cared for

Parents are your customers as well as the children

and benefits from attending your nursery, their perceptions of your service will also be influenced by the overall way in which you and your staff interact with them. Parental recommendation will be your most effective form of marketing for your nursery. Parental perceptions of your nursery are therefore extremely important.

From a business perspective, you will need to think about the parents as 'customers', view their expectations in terms of general 'customer service' and determine how your nursery can establish effective communication with parents to underpin and support your childcare service.

However, you will also need to recognise that there is an over-riding duty of care (under whichever piece of legislation governs your nursery – The Children Act and/or The Education Act) to safeguard the best interests and safety of the child, which should be the starting point for your childcare quality standards (addressed in Chapter 16).

WATCH POINT

Building and maintaining a strong reputation among parents is your best form of marketing.

CUSTOMER RETENTION – A BUSINESS PERSPECTIVE

Customer retention is vital to the success of any enterprise. This is a point worth remembering in all your dealings with the parents of children using your nursery.

Research indicates that businesses which have implemented successful

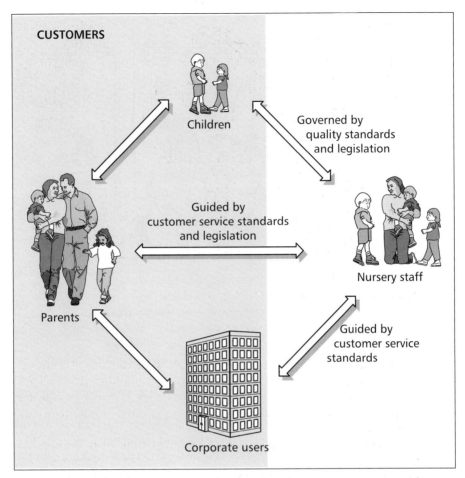

The basis of communications with customers of a nursery

customer retention strategies report that a 2 per cent improvement in retention has the same profit impact as a 10 per cent reduction in overheads. Thinking about this in terms of a nursery, if you have a nursery of 30 children, and one child leaves, this reduces your income by 3.33 per cent. If your fees are £130 per week, then the financial effect of a child leaving (and most likely leaving a vacancy for at least a month) is a monthly income loss of (£130 × 52) ÷ 12 = £563. If your profit margin is 10%, the corresponding reduction in profit margin is calculated as follows:

$$30 \times £563 \times 0.1 = £1689$$

$$(£563 \div £1689) \times 100 = 33.3\%$$

Here are five reasons why businesses find that keeping customers leads to better returns. Each of these reasons is applicable to a childcare business.

■ The cost of winning new customers is always more than we think (in fact, do we know how much it is?) – it includes advertising and publicity costs and

Customer retention is vital to the success of any enterprise

time invested in showing parents around the nursery.

- Loyal customers spend more on additional products and services, e.g. books, T-shirts, photographs, extra days or places for siblings.
- Retained customers are more willing to accept premium pricing – which may allow you to charge more than other nurseries offering a similar service.
- Customer maintenance costs are reduced, e.g. time spent communicating with disgruntled parents.
- Loyal customers build your reputation and image through word of mouth – this is the cheapest and most effective way of marketing a nursery.

The business message, then, is that customer service is important, and can affect the financial performance of your business.

However, the issues of customer retention must be balanced by your obligations to the children, and your childcare standards which will ultimately determine your stance on any particular issue.

By thinking about how you communicate with parents as customers, you should be able to ensure that you do not lose customers simply because they are dissatisfied with the way you have communicated with them. This especially applies to those sensitive occasions when you have to inform parents about an accident, or to discuss a health, behavioural or developmental problem relating to their child. You certainly do not want to lose customers because of a service issue which is peripheral to your core childcare service, e.g. being too heavy handed about late payment of fees, not returning telephone calls promptly or delays in answering correspondence.

WHAT IS CUSTOMER SERVICE?

In business terms customer service is a key element of any 'business offering'. The total offering to a customer comprises the core product or service, the additional service elements and the marketing intangibles. In terms of a nursery, these elements translate broadly as follows:

- Core product/service:
    Opening hours
    Ages of children
    Premises
    Childcare philosophy
    Nursery curriculum
    Programme for children
    Activities
    Overall standards of care, hygiene and safety
    Fees
- Additional service elements:
    Staff–parent interactions
    Parent–owner/manager interactions
    Pre-enrolment visits
    Accessibility
    Payment terms
    Support for families
- Marketing intangibles:
    Parental perceptions of your nursery

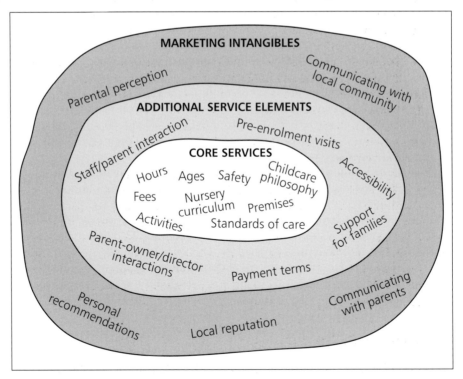

A nursery 'service offering'

Local reputation of your nursery
Communication with parents
Communication with the local community
Personal recommendations

In other words, the total offering to families using your nursery is not simply a description of the core childcare service – the nursery and the outcomes for the children. It encompasses additional service aspects and less tangible perceptions of your nursery, both of which you will also need to manage. An important part of this service is keeping parents informed about the nursery, their child's development and learning, interactions with other children and readiness for school.

HOW TO ACHIEVE A SUITABLE LEVEL OF CUSTOMER SERVICE

So what is it parents look for in terms of customer service? Clearly their first concern is for their child, and providing a suitably high standard of care should be your main focus of 'good customer service'. This is of over-riding importance, and should be governed by your quality standards.

What will parents be looking for in terms of additional services? Research indicates that customers generally have similar requirements of all organisations with which they have dealings. For a nursery these are:

■ sufficient and adequate information to enable them to fulfill their responsibilities and duties to their children. They have a right to know what your policies and practices are and the rationale behind them, how their child is developing, how their child's religion, language and culture are respected and reflected in the nursery programme etc.

■ easy and clear methods of communication with your organisation. They need to know with whom they should communicate on each type of matter, and how

■ responses which are sympathetic to the needs of their child – this is each parent's primary concern

■ a relationship which demonstrates that you see your role as part of a partnership working to produce the best outcomes, happiness and growth for their child

■ an opportunity for two-way dialogue – parents have a right to know what is happening in the nursery, and they generally like to be able to offer their views and have these listened to. This is an invaluable source of information for you to help you understand the parents' perceptions of your service

■ fast and appropriate responses to telephone calls or letters, e.g. they will expect letters to be acknowledged when received, even if you are not in a position to provide a detailed response initially.

Customer service in a nursery context, therefore, is largely about communication and how interactions with parents, including complaints or other problems, are handled. Communication and complaint handling are looked at in more detail in the next two sections of this chapter.

Communication with parents

Effective communication is vital in securing good customer service in a nursery. Parents have a right to be kept informed. This can also pre-empt dissatisfaction or complaints, and lead to feedback which will be valuable to you in shaping and improving your service.

Keeping the parents involved

THE VALUE OF COMMUNICATION

In terms of marketing it is worth remembering that there is no advantage unless it is communicated. You may consider your nursery to be the best in the area, but there is no advantage in this unless parents realise this too. They will make their own judgements from their own observations and the responses and progress of their child, but remember that parents generally only see the nursery at the beginning and end of their child's daily session, and they will not necessarily know what goes on during the day, or the things your staff do which are good practice or particularly innovative. Often it is worth taking the time and trouble to communicate some of these things to parents, through parents' letters, parents' evenings, bulletin boards or in person via your manager and staff. Never assume they know what you know. However, you should be careful not to focus on keeping the parents informed at the expense of spending time with the children, or of making demands on the children to produce a piece of work just to show parents.

You should be interested in feedback from parents about their needs and about your nursery, good and bad, so that you can develop your service further. Customer intelligence is something which large organisations value highly, but find it very difficult to get hold of (have you noticed how many customer questionnaires you have been asked to complete?). A nursery is in the very fortunate position of having twice daily personal contact with parents, making it relatively easy to get customer feedback, at least on an informal basis. You might also want to consider more formal mechanisms for achieving this, e.g. an annual parents' survey as part of your quality programme.

When reviewing feedback from parents, you should be careful not to give undue emphasis to any one particular view or perspective, and make sure that you take account of broader issues, equal opportunities, childcare standards etc.

Parents' expectations are likely to focus on their own child and their own way of life. As a matter of good communication you may need to explain to parents about the larger picture and professional standards. This should help them to understand better your policies and practices. Any changes you make in response to parental feedback must fit with your overall obligations, and the quality standards you need to address.

It is also worth remembering that private childcare is the subject of some political debate. In most communities, an élitist image is unlikely to be successful, so you need to be aware of possible tensions and coercive parents who wish to persuade other parents or staff to cause problems for your nursery simply because of their views on childcare.

INTERACTION WITH PARENTS

It is worth thinking about all the 'customer interactions' between your nursery and the parents. What information will you and parents want to exchange through each type of interaction? How should you or your staff respond to each type of interaction? What should you be doing to present a positive image of your nursery through that customer interaction? This can help clarify communication channels for parents and avoid misunderstandings. For example, if you expect most matters to be raised with the nursery manager, and only the most serious matters to be raised with you, or only those over which your manager has no control, then you should communicate this to parents so that they avoid by-passing the manager unnecessarily, but feel able to approach you directly when appropriate.

Typically the customer interactions in a nursery include the following:
■ initial telephone enquiry
■ first and any subsequent pre-enrolment visits to the nursery
■ admissions correspondence
■ prospectus, parents' leaflet and other information
■ enrolment visit
■ settling in days
■ morning and evening arrival and pick-up
■ daily conversations with staff – including informal discussion about the child's progress
■ specific discussion with the nursery manager and/or the child's key worker to discuss the child's progress, and areas of concern such as developmental delays, withdrawn or aggressive behaviour
■ specific discussions with the nursery manager on other matters
■ telephone calls or face-to-face contact to inform parents about any 'bumps' or more serious accidents

- telephone calls about any other matters
- administrative correspondence, including invoicing and payment of fees
- events at the nursery involving parents, children and staff
- visual displays presented for parent information
- nursery meetings for parents
- nursery newsletters for parents
- complaints
- correspondence when a child leaves.

These all represent opportunities to influence how the parents using your nursery feel about your nursery, your staff, you and the service you offer. It is therefore important that you think about the image you wish to present through these interactions, and how it would be most appropriate to relate to the parents as a partnership for the welfare of all the children and parents.

| | Parents ← → Staff | | | |
	Telephone	In person	Written	Visual
Pre-enrolment	Initial contact	Pre-enrolment visit	Leaflet and prospectus	First impressions of nursery
			Admissions correspondence	
		Enrolment and settling in	Parents' information booklet	
Daily contact		Morning and evening arrival and pick-up		Visual displays Parents' notice-board
		Informal discussion of child's progress		
Regular contact	Telephone calls to Manager	Specific discussions with Manager or Key Worker on child's progress	Administrative correspondence	
		Specific discussions with Manager on other matters		
Occasional contact	Information about accidents	Nursery events	Nursery newsletter	
		Information about accidents	Complaints	
		Parents' meetings/ evenings	Correspondence on leaving	
		Complaints		

Variety of interactions between parents and the nursery

The nursery prospectus and parents' information booklet are key to your communication with parents. The prospectus should set out your overall philosophy and what you are aiming to achieve in your nursery. It should also include formal 'terms and conditions' by which you expect parents to abide, detailing contractual points such as the nursery opening hours, when fees must be paid, when a child can be asked to leave the nursery etc.

The parents' information leaflet is your opportunity to explain in more detail about:

- the operation of the nursery
- your key worker (or equivalent) system
- the nursery routine
- how child profiles or other records are used
- child discipline
- health and safety
- accident and emergencies
- settling in
- what supplies to bring
- how parents can become involved in the nursery.

Both of these leaflets provide important information which parents need, and which can be used as a reference point, particularly if you have to deal with any difficult or controversial issues with parents.

SERVICE STANDARDS

If possible you should set some service standards, and ensure that your staff are aware of them. You should also make sure that these service standards fit with and support your childcare quality standards, equal opportunities policies and practices etc.

If necessary you should also offer your staff help and support in achieving these. For example, some staff may be unsure about how to answer the telephone, and what to say or do if the call is from a new parent enquiring about the nursery. You or your manager could offer guidance as to:

- how to answer the telephone helpfully, e.g. giving the name of the nursery rather than simply 'hello'
- whether they should take the parent's details and arrange to send a prospectus, or whether they should pass the call to the manager
- how they should describe the nursery and what information they should give. Are there any particular features of your nursery which make it different?
- what to do if someone wants to visit the nursery.

The kind of 'customer service' standards you may wish to set are:

- parents of ill or distressed children to be notified
- telephone calls to be returned with 24 hours
- letters to be answered or acknowledged within 3 days
- parents to be informed about serious accidents immediately
- nursery manager to be available for appointments with parents at reasonable notice.

People have different perceptions of parents' evenings

■ all complaints to be investigated within 7 days, and a written report produced. Parents' evenings are a potential minefield of misunderstanding. People have different perceptions of these evenings, so it is important to make their purpose clear, either through a newsletter or through your parents' information booklet. Is the evening intended to be purely social, or to provide information on a chosen theme, or for parents to discuss their child's progress with staff, or to raise particular issues with your manager or with you, or to invite a general discussion in open forum about the nursery? Unless you let parents know what to expect of these evenings, you may find that some will grow frustrated because the evenings are not achieving what they had hoped.

Complaints, accidents and other difficult issues

HANDLING COMPLAINTS

Effective complaint handling is very important to the maintenance of a business. It is worth viewing complaints in a positive light. Research indicates that a customer who complains and receives a satisfactory response is less likely to leave than a customer who has a grievance but does not complain. What this means is that parents who do not complain are actually more at risk of leaving than parents who do complain. You may well find that a parent who complains and receives a satisfactory and appropriate response becomes an even more loyal supporter of your nursery than previously.

Customers who complain are more valuable than those who do not

WATCH POINT

The best customers are often those who complain – you can do something to address their grievances.

However, you should also bear in mind that some parents are persistent complainers, or attempt to make political points through complaining to the nursery.

As part of the registration requirements for your nursery, you will be required to have a complaints policy. This policy (along with others) should be clarified in a parents' information leaflet or in the contract with parents. It must include reference to the local authority inspection unit, to which all complaints can ultimately be referred.

It is impossible to predict the nature of complaints – each one is different – and how you respond will depend on the specific complaint. In some cases parents may have genuine grounds for complaint; in others they may have misunderstood a situation or have been misinformed, and there are parents who simply like complaining. You will need to judge each situation individually and respond accordingly, but there are some ways in which you can prepare yourself for handling complaints, and these should be reflected in your complaints procedure:

- be prepared to listen to parents when they complain, and to see this as an opportunity not as a problem
- be sure of your quality standards, the impression given in your literature and your legal obligations
- think about what kind of issues you might expect parents to raise, and investigate how you could make parents aware of this, perhaps through your prospectus, in a parents' information leaflet or in a complaints procedure

- implement a procedure to acknowledge complaints immediately, even if you are not able to provide an immediate response
- set yourself a target time-scale for dealing with complaints
- train and support your manager and the nursery staff and allow them to be able to address minor problems immediately and effectively. Help them to be confident, supportive, trained and knowledgeable. Be sure that staff are not able to shift responsibility or 'cover up'
- make it clear to your manager how and when you would like to be kept informed of complaints, and on what type of issues
- keep a record of complaints – and of compliments, to make sure you get the balance right
- motivate your staff (and yourself) to view complaint handling positively as a means of building loyalty from families using the nursery.

When confronted with a complaint about a member of staff, you should not jump to conclusions. If you have been wise in your staff appointments and have a good communication system you should know your staff well enough to understand the circumstances which may have led to the complaint. You must be sure that neither you nor the parents treat your member of staff in a way which could lead them to claim constructive dismissal or defamation of character. Of course the member of staff may be guilty of gross negligence or gross misconduct and then you must take urgent action on the parent's complaint.

WATCH POINTS

- Put the child first in all of your discussions with parents.
- Nurture and protect your nursery's reputation in every way.
- Identify the different ways in which the nursery has contact with parents, and make sure you are giving the intended impression.
- Think about the service standards parents expect, especially to support their lives as working parents. Do what you can to match these standards.
- React positively to complaints or negative feedback, and learn from them.
- Communicate, communicate, communicate – this is the best way to involve parents, avoid misunderstandings and keep the valuable support of the parents using your nursery.

OTHER DIFFICULT ISSUES

Apart from complaints, you will almost certainly find there are other difficult issues you have to address with parents. These might involve telling parents about an accident involving their child, other incidents such as bite marks on their child, broken or stolen possessions, and a range of other issues.

In such circumstances it may help to remember the tips given to people in large organisations who deal with the media when there is a problem:

- say you are sorry this has happened
- explain why it has happened

- give information about what will happen next
- offer support and help as appropriate.

Because of your responsibility for the welfare of the child, you may have to face up to some highly sensitive conversations with parents. Parents and children's interests are not always the same.

Your best approach to most issues is likely to be through the concept of shared care between parents and the nursery, and the honesty and partnership which will be good for the child. In this way, concerns such as developmental delay, disability, anti-social behaviour etc. can be dealt with in a way which shows respect for parents and does not alienate them.

It is conceivable that you may have to discuss with parents concerns about child abuse or neglect. You may find this difficult and you will need to be fairly certain of your facts, and in contact with Social Services. However, you cannot avoid declaring your concerns.

Such discussions may not be appreciated by parents and can cause disquiet. However, you have a primary obligation to the children in your care. If you act responsibly, this will be recognised and ultimately will enhance your reputation in serving children's best interests.

An up-front equal opportunities policy should be sufficient to guard against any parents behaving in a racist or sexist manner to other parents or to staff. It should also help to discourage parents from encouraging racism or sexism in their child. However, you will, undoubtedly, from time to time, have to address the issues of racism and sexism. Just remember that most parents will respect your stance, and your record will reassure potential customers.

Conclusion

Dealing with parents is not easy. They are usually highly sensitive to the welfare and safety of their child, and are understandingly demanding in this respect. They may also be finding it difficult to balance the demands of work and family if they are employed, and this can influence their interactions with your nursery.

There may be times when you have to raise issues with parents which they are not happy to hear, or where their desires, preferences or behaviour are at odds with your legal obligations and responsibilities to the child.

By thinking carefully about your communication with parents, how you would like this to take place, what information you would like to exchange, how you would like parents to perceive your nursery, and how you will tackle difficult issues, you will be able to avoid many problems, and build loyal support which will bring long-term benefits to your nursery.

CHECKLIST

Define what you are offering
- Product
- Service
- Intangibles

CHECKLIST continued

Identify parent–nursery interactions

- Initial telephone enquiry
- First and any subsequent pre-enrolment visits to the nursery
- Admissions correspondence
- Enrolment visit
- Settling in days
- Morning and evening arrival and pick-up
- Daily conversations between parents and staff
- Specific discussions between parents and the nursery manager
- Specific discussions between parents and the child's key worker
- Telephone calls
- Administrative correspondence
- Events at the nursery involving parents, children and staff
- Parents' evenings
- Parents' letters
- Complaints
- Correspondence when a child leaves

Service standards

- Image
- Telephone
- Correspondence
- Complaint handling
- Staff training and support

Plan communication

- Information
- Method
- Frequency

16 QUALITY MATTERS

> **What this chapter covers:**
> ■ Children's rights
> ■ Baselines
> ■ Systematic approaches
> ■ Managing for quality

Mankind owes to the child the best it has to give.

United Nations Declaration

The focus of this chapter is a clarification of aspects of 'quality', because so much is spoken and written about the importance of quality standards in nurseries. It suggests action which can help to demonstrate quality standards and introduces the growing body of regulatory systems which attempt to assure levels of quality.

There is general agreement that good quality provision ensures that children will benefit from attending a nursery. There is also general consensus about the fundamental expectations of quality in early years provision. However, more precise descriptions about what constitutes quality, and how it can best be achieved and measured, vary. This is largely because quality is value based and depends on the perspective from which it is being examined.

For the nursery provider the establishment of quality standards is a primary task. A broad-based, balanced and up-to-date perspective is recommended to inform the setting of standards. To set the quality standards for your nursery, the baseline statutory regulations should be augmented by other professional and academic views of quality as well as the views of relevant partners including the staff, parents and the children themselves.

A focus on quality issues is a common feature of management generally and, therefore, it is not surprising that there is a considerable body of existing views and written material about the management of quality in business and industry. Nursery managers may usefully take this guidance on board. However, they should be wary of the pitfalls of applying ideas which are too much geared to products and commercial success. For example, guaranteeing identical widgets is highly desirable in industry, keeping customers happy is good news in sales, but honestly tackling the individual needs of children and families is the essence of good nursery provision.

Quality standards are intended to be operational, to be controlled and maintained over time. Consequently, it is necessary to be able to monitor standards in practice. In addition, the very nature of quality dictates that practice should be refined, improved and enriched. It is important to take account of the insights and values continually emerging from research, academic publications and professional bodies. This leads to quality improvement.

Children's rights

The most critical elements of quality encompass children's rights and needs. These include:

- the right to be protected from physical or emotional neglect, physical or emotional abuse, accidents which could have long-term negative effects and unnecessary exposure to risks, infections, etc.
- the right to a healthy life, with care and treatment provided as necessary, good nutrition and opportunities for physical development
- the right to a stable caring and learning environment and to positive relationships with adult carers and educators
- the right to self-esteem as an individual, to have affection and love, to experience dignity and respect and to develop autonomy
- the right to experience self-confidence and enjoyment in learning, to have opportunities for self-expression and to develop language, skills, and knowledge
- the right to experience friendships and co-operation with others, to develop social skills and to develop positive ways of relating to other people of all ages
- the right to equal opportunities irrespective of gender, race, or disability; and to experience cultural diversity
- the right to support and inclusion as part of a family; and to be part of a community
- the right to be happy.

Baselines

The starting point for establishing nursery quality has to be the regulations which are set out in Volume 2 of *The Guidance to The Children Act* and the local authority nursery registration requirements. The requirements, although set at a minimum level, are intended to lead to good childcare standards. The registration process incorporates a number of stages and approvals by all the relevant statutory officers. It is worth remembering that it may be appropriate for you to suggest alternative options in line with your views and business plan. However, the statutory authorities have to balance your needs against legal frameworks, and what is ultimately thought to be in the overall best of interests of children and their families.

Other baseline standards are linked to the nursery learning programme which will require that a body of established frameworks and standards are adhered to. These will arise in addition to the registration regulations. Further, there are likely to be particular attitudes and practices which you want to follow in order to deliver the type of service you feel is appropriate or to differentiate your nursery from others. All these are components of quality and will form part of the baseline for your nursery's quality standards.

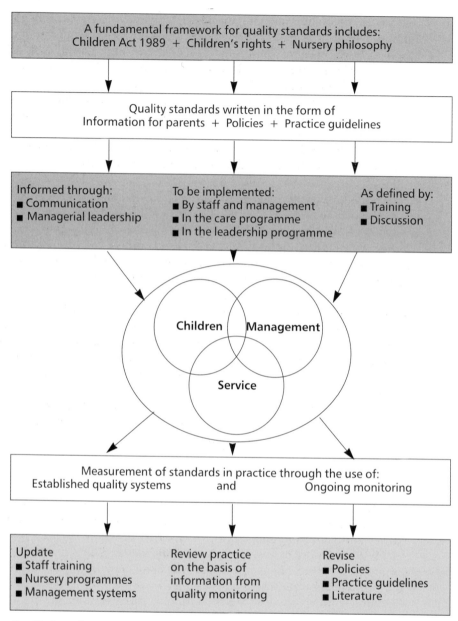

A fundamental framework for quality standards includes:
Children Act 1989 + Children's rights + Nursery philosophy

Quality standards written in the form of
Information for parents + Policies + Practice guidelines

Informed through:
■ Communication
■ Managerial leadership

To be implemented:
■ By staff and management
■ In the care programme
■ In the leadership programme

As defined by:
■ Training
■ Discussion

Children | Management

Service

Measurement of standards in practice through the use of:
Established quality systems   and   Ongoing monitoring

Update
■ Staff training
■ Nursery programmes
■ Management systems

Review practice
on the basis of
information from
quality monitoring

Revise
■ Policies
■ Practice guidelines
■ Literature

Quality in action

QUALITY STANDARDS AND STATEMENTS

To underpin the operation of a quality programme it is necessary to frame written quality standards. The standards form the basis of the contents of the nursery policies, the prospectus and parent information literature. They must also be the basis for much of the in-service training of staff. Statements can include aims for outcomes as well as descriptions of service provision.

The development of a body of written policies, forms, plans and checklists is a key activity in establishing quality and quality control and monitoring systems. It may sound impractical or laborious to write things out in detail, but there is a clear benefit in terms of having to get to grips with specific actions and to think through the process of how standards are to be established and maintained.

A wide circulation of written documentation is essential if standards are to be understood by all those involved, if they are to be monitored over time and if they are to be updated as new knowledge or experience dictates.

QUALITY CONTROL AND QUALITY MONITORING

Ultimately, the achievement of good quality provision relies on the baseline quality standards being incorporated into daily practice and being maintained consistently. Quality control is about ensuring that the promised standards are met. This can be measured through regular quality monitoring.

In order to monitor quality effectively, a range of tools is needed. Some are an intrinsic part of specific quality systems. These are mainly based on observation, assessment and feedback by an independent person working within a formal framework. Others are more informal and depend largely on the development of significant opportunities for discussion and general communication amongst all the nursery's interested parties – management, staff, parents and children. There are still other tools to be found within the plethora of the nursery's own general records. When and how each type of tool is employed is related to the system or systems governing the nursery's quality and the ways in which quality is being managed in the nursery.

QUALITY ENHANCEMENT AND IMPROVEMENT

Improvements in quality should develop naturally. Regular reviews of the standards, input from staff and parents, independent inspections, new research and publications addressing quality issues are some of the factors which will lead to recognition of ways to improve quality. This will lead to the enhancement of some existing standards, alongside the development of new standards, with their contingent policies, records and monitoring features.

Systematic approaches

Quality matters thrive on systematic approaches. There are a number of options from which to choose. These range from the regulatory or statutory, through the personal/subjective, to the scientific. As providers will realise, there are limitations and strengths to each type of system. Some are more easily managed than others. There are also cost considerations. Using a combination of two or three systems is likely to be of the most benefit to the nursery.

QUALITY MONITORING SYSTEM

Standard to be monitored	Maintain a 1:3 staff:child ratio at all times for all children under 2 years old			
One day only critical times snapshot view	Date:_____ Location:_____			

Time	No. of children present	No. of staff on duty		Resulting ratio
		Qualified	Unqualified	
8:00 a.m.				
8:30 a.m.				
9:00 a.m.				
9:30 a.m.				
10:00 a.m.				
———				
4:00 p.m.				
4:30 p.m.				
5:00 p.m.				
5:30 p.m.				
6:00 p.m.				

Monitored by:_____ Job title: _____ Date:_____

Seen by manager:_____ Date:_____

Seen by quality manager:_____ Date:_____

Comments:_____

_____

Example of a form for monitoring staff : child ratios

QUALITY MONITORING SYSTEM

Standard to be monitored	Keyworker will provide special support and continuity for the child

One week only critical times snapshot view

Week beginning:_____
Location:_____
Keyworker: _____
Child: _____

Interaction	Monday		Tuesday		Wednesday		Thursday		Friday	
	a.m.	p.m.	a.m.	p.m.	a.m.	p.m.	a.m.	p.m.	a.m.	p.m.
Present at arrival										
Talked to parent or carer										
Shared the same activity										
Supervised lunch										
Supervised sleep										
Shared the same activity										
Observations for assessment										
Planned a special activity										
Shared a cuddle										
Shared a joke										
Shared a storybook										
Present at collection										
Talked to parent or carer										

Additional comments: _____

Monitored by:_____ Title:_____ Date:_____

Seen by manager:_____ Date:_____

Seen by quality manager:_____ Date:_____

Comments:_____

Example of a form for monitoring keyworker support

REGISTRATION UNDER THE CHILDREN ACT 1989

As described previously, the initial registration of a nursery by the designated local authority officers is required to allow the nursery to open. The registration standards are based on the document 'Family Support, Day Care and Educational Provision for Young Children' which is Volume 2 of the Guidance to The Children Act 1989 and the officers also must also have due regard to other relevant legislation. The process of registration is fairly rigorous and can take up to six months to be completed. A standard fee is charged. Particular emphasis is placed on the range of legal responsibilities such as those relating to fire safety, environmental health, food handling, child health and child protection. An equal emphasis is also placed on the development of policies and practice related to professional quality issues. Registration stipulates the requirements for a 'fit person' to be in charge of the nursery, adult/child supervision ratios, equal opportunities, record keeping, management structures and outcomes for children. Annual inspections are intended to ensure that the required minimum standards are being maintained. Additional help, encouragement, training opportunities, etc. may be offered as a way of improving on quality. Being registered and inspected is an unavoidable legal requirement, but the process also offers a helpful independent assessment on which your nursery can build.

THE NURSERY EDUCATION GRANT

The basic requirements of the nursery education grant scheme are set out in the Nursery Education and Grant Maintained Schools Act 1996. To participate in the scheme (originally the Nursery Voucher Scheme), nursery settings must agree to be rigorously inspected by specially trained OFSTED Inspectors. The inspection is evidence based against a framework set by OFSTED. Inspectors take a view on the extent to which the nursery's planning, teaching, assessment and resourcing is likely to promote the Desirable Learning Outcomes for children by the time they reach compulsory school age. Guides published by the DfEE set out the criteria to be used in inspections and indicate the process to be followed and the documentation required. Inspections take place at two- to four-year intervals unless specific problems have been identified by the inspectors. The inspections, related self-assessment forms and follow-up action plans are based on well-established principles and consequently are highly useful as a quality system.

PROVIDER'S OBSERVATIONS

The traditional, personalised and subjective approach is one in which the nursery manager/proprietor oversees every aspect of the nursery, closely supervises staff activity and has a general 'feeling' about how things are going. On a daily basis, through being on the premises, it is possible to make assessments of the quality being offered and to take action to improve services as observed to be necessary. When there are only a few cries from babies, children are settled-in quickly, the developmental progress of children fits within the standard expectations, the accident rate is minimal, there is very little turnover of staff, the daily routine fulfils a range of expectations and parents have few complaints, the manager can take the view that the nursery is achieving a reasonable standard.

PARENTAL FEEDBACK

This is another traditional and personal approach in which parents are encouraged to use a variety of informal and formal means to express their views and influence the nursery programme. Opportunities may be limited to daily chats with staff at dropping-off or collection time, or they may include a parents' committee, parents' evenings or written surveys. The parental involvement may centre on the perceived needs of their own children, or may extend (even in the private sector) to staff recruitment, the finances and business plan. Comments, suggestions and complaints from parents are accepted as significant indicators of the degree to which quality standards are being achieved.

BRITISH STANDARDS INSTITUTE (BSI)

Achieving registration by the BSI involves a detailed, usually lengthy and sometimes costly process. The focus of the ISO 9000 (formerly BS 5750) framework is to ensure predictable conformity in outcomes or products. To do this, the nursery management agree a set of childcare and management standards based on working practices, set within the BSI framework. The involvement of every level of the work force is required. Performance is regularly measured against the agreed, planned detailed set of actions, and monitored through a system of record keeping. The BSI carry out thorough annual inspections and the BSI kite mark represents a guarantee of a declared standard of quality.

INVESTORS IN PEOPLE (IIP)

Being able to display the IIP logo signals the status of an organisation which has taken the view that a planned and developed programme of ongoing staff training is an investment rather than a cost to the budget. Recognition as an IIP organisation is a formal process which requires a demonstration of public commitment to regular training for all staff and management, with evaluation of outcomes and follow-up action to ensure effectiveness. The key concept is that well-trained staff can offer a higher quality, more efficient, customer-focused, service. Guidance and Recognition Panels for achieving IIP status come mainly via local Training and Enterprise Councils (TECs). There are undoubtedly financial implications to maintaining the training programme, but some help may be available through the TEC.

EARLY CHILDHOOD ENVIRONMENT RATING SCALE (ECERS)

ECERS, an American system of rating scales, was developed basically as a tool for research. It has been used internationally in a number of different childcare settings to look objectively and academically at the quality of, broadly defined, environmental aspects of the facilities offered. Training and experience in its use is essential, in order to sensibly apply the seven possible numerical ratings (inadequate to excellent). Ratings are assessed on the basis of two- to three-hour long observations of a range of topic areas, including: personal care routines, furnishings and displays, language, reasoning experiences, fine and gross motor activities, creative activities, social development and adult needs.

Managing for quality

Quality is not separate from the general day to day running of the nursery. Whatever quality systems are adopted, the degree to which standards are achieved and maintained is directly affected by the management arrangements and the sensitive leadership of the nursery manager and proprietor. Taking the lead on quality is a major and relentless aspect of the overall managerial responsibility.

Managing for quality is a complex process. It requires an understanding of the interplay between values, standards, policies, management structures, environment and ethos, record keeping, communication strategies and so on.

AN EXAMPLE OF MANAGEMENT OF A QUALITY STANDARD

The nursery will ensure continuity of care for each child.

1. Written lists of children and their keyworkers, drawn up periodically and kept on file, will show any changes which have taken place in keyworker allocations. How frequent have changes been and for what reasons? Could an early temporary change in keyworker have been avoided if the child had been allocated to a different carer because the keyworker's holiday was anticipated at the time of the child's enrolment? Could a change have been avoided at an early or critical point because a staff member's resignation was anticipated? Would it have been more beneficial for an established keyworker to take on the (extra) responsibility for the new child as a transition to phasing out responsibility for another child who was well settled and could cope with a change? What opportunities were there for staff members and parents to explore the implications of change and to contribute to the decisions taken?

2. Reference to individual child profile/assessment records or baby diaries could provide insights about significant achievements, milestones, educational progress or new behaviour patterns linked to changes in keyworker. What do they signal about the child's reaction to the change? Do they suggest that there were compensating factors, such as being changed to a

keyworker with whom they already had an established relationship? Did this work for the child? Who was responsible for making observations and adding to the records? What opportunities were there for staff and parents to monitor the child's needs and link those into the planning mechanisms?

3. A comparative look at the written record of staff shift patterns and the child attendance register should throw up information about what the communication and hand-over/collection arrangements are for the child. If the keyworker is rarely present at the time when parents arrive or collect, what sort of continuity is possible? Who is providing the continuity with the parents? How is this affecting the child's care and development? And do the manager's working hours facilitate easy contact with the parents, who might wish to update details or discuss important and confidential matters?

4. The daily routine for the nursery should be looked at alongside the daily staff duty rota, and the record of the activity programme. From these plans and records it is possible to sensibly examine the interruptions to the child/keyworker time together. Is there sufficient time, on a daily basis, for the keyworker and child interaction to be beneficial to the child? What possible adjustments could be made in the routine and rota to facilitate more time together, especially when the child is ill or distressed? What adjustments could be made to allow for other staff to support a keyworker who is not feeling well herself or when the child is going through a 'difficult' phase – so that the child is not short changed? Is the day organised so that the child has time to enjoy a special relationship with a member of staff?

Conclusion

Quality matters are complex and value based. The minimum standards are those set out in the local authority registration requirements. Nevertheless, having a clear vision of what is meant by 'quality', and a baseline for operations, are prerequisites for setting and maintaining quality standards for your nursery. There are a number of different systems which can be used to inform quality management. Some will be more appropriate than others and they may be used in combination with each other to be the most effective.

Information about quality standards and systems is available from a variety of sources including those in the statutory, voluntary and commercial sectors. There are useful books and other documents to advise providers, as well as consultants who will (for a fee) offer tailor-made guidance on quality matters. The local authority, TECs, DfEE, OFSTED and BSI are reliable early contacts.

CHECKLIST

Registration under The Children Act
■ Planning and building
■ Fire safety

CHECKLIST continued

- Environmental health
- Operational plans and policies

Written policies
- Childcare and learning
- Equal opportunities
- Health and safety
- Accidents
- Complaints
- Administration of medicines
- Behaviour management
- Children with special needs

Staff matters
- Contracts of employment
- References
- Proof of qualifications
- Police checks
- Profile of staff experience
- The fit person
- Qualified First Aiders
- Training and development plan

Management information
- Numbers and ages of children
- Adult:child ratios
- Nursery opening hours
- Details of fees and parent contracts
- Information for parents
- Daily routine
- Planning for the learning programme
- Child records
- Insurance cover
- Financial plan

Managing quality
- Standards
- Statements
- Systems
- Monitoring tools
- Controls and review
- Improvements and enhancement
- Communication and training strategies

Principles underpinning quality
- Children's rights
- Children Act Guidance
- Parental partnerships
- Staff involvement

USEFUL ADDRESSES AND SOURCES OF INFORMATION

Financial, business and legal

British Chambers of Commerce, Manning House, 22 Carlisle Place, London SW1P 1JA, 0171 565 2000.

British Venture Capital Association, 12 Essex Street, London WC2 3AA, 0171 240 3846.

Business in the Community, 44 Baker Street, London W1M 1DH, 0171 224 1600.

Business Link Signpost Line (for information about local Business Link offices) 0345 567 765.

Companies Registration Office, Companies House, Crown Way, Maindy, Cardiff CF4 3UZ, 0122 235 8588.

Confederation of British Industry, Centrepoint, 103 New Oxford Street, London WC1A 1DU, 0171 379 7400.

Data Protection Register, Wycliffe House, Water Lane, Wilmslow, Cheshire, SK9 5AF, 0162 554 5745.

Department of Trade and Industry, 1 Victoria Street, London SW1H 0ET, 0171 215 5000.

Institute of Chartered Accountants in England and Wales, Moorgate Place, London EC2, 0171 920 8100.

Institute for Independent Businesses, Clarendon House, 33 Bridle Path, Watford WD2 4AA, 01923 239 543.

Loan Guarantee Scheme, Department of Trade and Industry, St Mary's House, Moorfoot, Sheffield S1 4PQ, 01142 597 308.

London Enterprise Agency, 4 Snow Hill, London EC1A 2BS, 0171 236 3000.

National Federation of Self-employed and Small Businesses, 32 Orchard Road, Lytham St Anne's, Lancs FY8 1NY, 0125 372 0911.

National Private Day Nurseries Association, Portland House, 55 New Hey Road, Lindley, Huddersfield HD3 4AL, 01484 546 502.

Prince's Youth Business Trust, 18 Park Square East, London NW1 4LH, 0171 543 1234.

Small Business Publications, Freephone 0800 777 888, or contact a branch of National Westminster Bank PLC.

The Law Society, 113 Chancery Lane, London WC2, 0171 242 1222.

The Small Firms Service, Department of Trade and Industry, 1 Victoria Street, London SW1H 0ET, 0171 215 5000.

Employment, health and safety

ACAS (Advisory, Conciliation and Arbitration Service), 83 Euston Road, London NW1 2RB, 0171 396 0022.

British Red Cross, 9–10 Grosvenor Crescent, London SW1X 7EJ, 0171 235 5454.

CRE (Commission for Racial Equality), Elliot House, 10/12 Allington Street, London SW1E 5EH, 0171 828 7022.

DfEE (Department for Education and Employment), Sanctuary Buildings, Great Smith Street, London SW1P 3BT, 0171 925 5000.

EOC (Equal Opportunities Commission), Overseas House, Quay Street, Manchester M3 3HN, 0161 833 9244.

Gee Publishing Limited, 100 Avenue Road, London NW3 3PG, 0171 393 7400.

Health & Safety Executive Books, PO Box 199, Sudbury, Suffolk CO10 6FS, 0178 788 1165.

HSE (Health & Safety Executive) Information Centre, Broad Lane, Sheffield SH3 7HQ, 01541 545500.

IPD (Institute of Personnel and Development), 35 Camp Road, London SW19, 0181 971 9000.

Local Authorities National Joint Councils Secretaries, 41 Belgrave Square, London SW1, 0171 235 6081.

NCVCCO (National Council of Voluntary Child Care Organisations), Unit 4, Pride Court, 80–82 White Lion Street, London N1 9PF, 0171 833 3319.

ROSPA (Royal Society for the Prevention of Accidents),353 Bristol Road, Birmingham B5 7ST, 0121 248 2000.

St John's Ambulance, 1 Grosvenor Crescent, London SW1X 7EF, 0171 235 5231.

The Industrial Society, 3 Carlton House Terrace, London SW1, 0171 839 4300.

The Stationery Office (formerly HMSO). Book shops located in London, Belfast, Birmingham, Bristol and Manchester. General enquiries 0171 873 0011.

Local contacts

The Local Authority Registration and Inspection Unit and your local Chamber of Commerce are good places to start to obtain the information you need. They will be equipped with standard literature and forms which you will need to start up your nursery.

Other useful local contacts include:

Business Link offices (there is a network of offices throughout the country).

Community College.

Enterprise Agency.

Health promotion department of Local Health Authority.

Job Centre.

Library.

Local Authority Early Years Department (may be based in Social Services or Education Department).

Local Authority Registration and Inspection Unit.
Social Security and Benefits Office.
TEC (local Training and Enterprise Council).
Voluntary Service Council.

Childcare and education

BAECE (British Association for Early Childhood Education), 111 City View House, 463 Bethnal Green Road, London E2 9QY 0171 739 7594.

CAPT (Child Accident Prevention Trust), Clerks Court, 18–20 Farringdon Lane, London EC1R 3AU, 0171 608 3828.

Child Education (magazine), Scholastic Limited, Westfield Road, Southam, Leamington Spa, Warwickshire CV3 30BR, 01926 813 910.

Childcare Business (magazine), Datateam Publishing Limited, Datateam House, Tovill Hill, Maidstone, Kent ME15 6QS, 01622 687 031.

Community Transport Association, Highbank, Halton Street, Hyde, Cheshire SK14 2NY, 0161 367 8780.

DfEE (Department for Education and Employment), Sanctuary Buildings, Great Smith Street, London SW1P 3BT, 0171 925 5055/6.

DfEE Publication Centre, PO Box 6927, London E3 3NZ, 0171 510 0150.

EYTARN (Early Years Trainers Anti-racist Network), PO Box 1870, London N12 8JQ, 0181 446 7056.

Foundation for the Study of Infant Deaths (cot death research and support), 14 Halkin Street, London SW1, 0171 235 0965.

Health Education Authority, Hamilton House, Mabledon Place, London WC1H 9TX.

High Scope Institute, Copperfield House, 190–192 Maple Road, London SE20 8HT, 0181 676 0220.

London Montessori Centre, 18 Balderton Street, London W1Y 1TG, 0171 493 0165.

Montessori St. Nicholas Centre, 23 Princes Gate, London, SW7, 0171 225 1277.

National Childbirth Trust, Alexandra House, Oldham Terrace, London W3 6NH, 0181 992 8637.

National Children's Bureau, 8 Wakely Street, London EC1V 7QE, 0171 278 6441.

National Early Years Network, 77 Holloway Road, London, N7 8JZ, 0171 607 9573.

National Playing Fields Association, 25 Ovington Square, London SW3, 0171 584 6445.

National Private Day Nurseries Association, Portland House, 55 New Hey Road, Lindley, Huddersfield HD3 4AL, 01484 546 502.

Nursery World (magazine), Vector Court, 151–153 Farringdon Road, London EC1R 2AD, 0171 278 7669.

OFSTED (Office for Standards in Education), Alexander House, 29–33 Kingsway, London WC2B 6SE, 0171 421 6800.

OFSTED Publications Centre, PO Box 6927, London E3 3NZ, 0171 510 0180.

Parents at Work, Fifth Floor, Beech Street, Barbican, London EC2Y 8AD, 0171 628 3565.

Play Group Network, PO Box 23, Whitley Bay, Tyne & Wear NE26 3DB.

Play Matters/National Toy and Leisure Libraries, 68 Churchway, London NW1 1LT, 0171 387 9592.

Pre-school Learning Alliance, 61–63 Kings Cross Road, London WC1X 9LL, 0171 833 0991.

Steiner Waldorf Schools Fellowship, Kidbroke Park, Forest Row, Sussex RH18 5JB, 01342 822115.

The Daycare Trust, Wesley House, 4 Wild Court, London EC1R 3AU, 0171 405 5617.

The Food Commission, 3rd Floor, 5–11 Worship Street, London EC2A 2BH, 0171 628 7774.

The Stationery Office Publications Centre (formerly HMSO), PO Box 276, London SW8 5DT, 0171 873 9090 (orders), 0171 873 0011 (enquiries).

Times Educational Supplement (newspaper), Admiral House, 66–68 East Smithfield, London E1 9XY, 0171 782 3000.

Suppliers

Baby Basics, PO Box 801, Chippenham, Wiltshire SN14 6JB, 01249 449 123. Baby equipment.

Community Insight, The Pembroke Centre, Chemey Manor, Swindon, SN2 2PQ, 01793 512 612. Books on childcare and education as well as children's books.

Community Playthings, Robertsbridge, East Sussex TN32 5DR, 0800 387 457. Mainly wooden furniture and equipment.

Galt Educational, Culvert Street, Oldham, Lancs OL4 2ST, 0161 627 5086. Range includes wooden furniture.

GLS Fairway Limited, Ferry Lane, Tottenham Hale, London N17 9NQ, 0181 801 3333. Wide range including stationery and office equipment, catering equipment and art supplies.

Letterbox Library, Leroy House, Essex Road, London, N1, 0171 220 1633. Multi-cultural and non-sexist children's books.

Montessori St. Nicholas Learning Materials, PO Box 390, Wetherby, Yorks LS23 7LR, 01937 840 230.

Montessori Trading Company Limited, 121 College Road, London, NW10 5EY, 0181 960 7585. Equipment for Montessori programmes.

NES Arnold Limited, Ludlow Hill Road, West Bridgford, Nottingham, NG2 6HD, 0115 945 2201. Wide range of nursery equipment including art materials, multi-cultural items and baby equipment.

OYEZ Stationery Group, 144 Fetter Lane, London, EC4, 0171 405 2847. Legal forms.

Seton Limited, PO Box 77, Banbury, Oxon OX16 7LS, 0800 585 501. Safety equipment, signs and identification.

Viking Direct, Burson Industrial Park, Tollwell Road, Leicester, LE4 1BR, 0800 424 444. Office supplies.

Waterlow Business Supplies, Bletchley, Milton Keynes MK1 1UJ, 01908 361 111. Personnel record forms.

WESCO, 114 Highfields Road, Witham, Essex CM8 2HH, 01376 503 590. Range includes soft play shapes and outdoor activity equipment.

FURTHER READING

Framework for nursery provision

Department of Health, The Children Act 1989, *Guidance and Regulations, Volume 2: Family Support, Day Care and Educational Provision for Young Children*, HMSO, 1991

Department for Education and Employment and Schools Curriculum and Assessment Authority, *Desirable Outcomes for Children's Learning*, DfEE, 1996

National Children's Bureau, *Young Children in Group Daycare: Guidelines for Good Practice*, NCB, 1994

National Early Years Network, *Education and the under eights: a guide to the law*, Starting Points No 22, NEYN, 1997

Wild, N., *Responsibility for under eights: a guide to the law*, Starting Points No 23, NEYN, 1996

Childcare and education

Athey, C., *Extending Thought in Young Children*, Paul Chapman Publishing, 1990

Blenkin, G. and Kelly, A.V., *Early Childhood Education: A Developmental Curriculum*, Paul Chapman Publishing, 1992

Blenkin, G. and Kelly, A.V., *Assessment in Early Childhood Education: A Developmental Curriculum*, Paul Chapman Publishing, 1992

Brown, B., *All Our Children: a guide for those who care*, BBC, 1996

Bruce, T., *Early Childhood Education*, Hodder & Stoughton, 1987

Commission for Racial Equality, *From cradle to school: A practical guide to race equality and childcare*, CRE, 1996

Dare, A. and O'Donovan, M., *A Practical Guide to Working with Babies*, Stanley Thornes, 1994

Dare, A. and O'Donovan, M., *Good Practice in Caring for Young Children with Special Needs*, Stanley Thornes, 1997

Derman-Sparks, L. and the A.B.C. Task Force, *Anti-Bias Curriculum: Tools for Empowering Young Children*, National Association for the Education of Young Children, 1989

Drummond, M. J., *Assessing Children's Learning*, David Fulton, 1993

Elfer, P., *With Equal Concern*, National Children's Bureau, 1995

Finch, S., *Computers in Early Years Settings: an Introduction*, Starting Points No 24, National Early Years Network, 1997

Goldschmeid, E. and Jackson, S., *People Under Three*, Routledge, 1994

Holiman, M. and Weikart, D.P., *Educating Young Children*, High Scope Press, 1995

Hurst, V., *Planning for Early Learning*, Second Edition, Paul Chapman Publishing, 1997

Hutchin, V., *Tracking Significant Achievement in the Early Years*, Hodder & Stoughton, 1996

Lally, M., *The Nursery Teacher in Action*, Paul Chapman Publishing, 1991

Lindon, J., *Child Development from Birth to Eight: A Practical Focus*, National Children's Bureau, 1993

Mason, M., *Inclusion, the way forward: A guide to integration for young disabled children*, Starting Points No 15, National Early Years Network, 1993

Millam, R., *Anti-Discriminatory Practice: A Guide for Workers in Childcare and Education*, Cassell, 1996

Montessori, M., *The Absorbent Mind*, Clio Press Ltd

Moss, P. and Pence, A., *Valuing Quality in Early Childhood Services*, Paul Chapman Publishing, 1994

National Association of Toy and Leisure Libraries, and BBC Magazine, *The Good Toy Guide*, BBC, published annually

Neaum, S. and Tallack, J., *Good Practice in Implementing the Pre-school Curriculum*, Stanley Thornes, 1997

Nutbrown, C., *Threads of Thinking: Young Children Learning and the Role of Early Education*, Paul Chapman Publishing, 1994

Pinset, P., *Language, Culture and Young Children: Developing English in the Multi-ethnic Nursery and Infant School*, David Fulton Publishers Ltd, 1992

Pugh, G., *Contemporary Issues in the Early Years*, National Children's Bureau 1992

Rudel, J. and Rudel, S., *Education Towards Freedom*, Lanthorn Press, 1972 (Note: This book is recommended by the Steiner Waldorf Schools Fellowship)

The Rumbold Report, *Starting with Quality: The Report of the Committee of Enquiry into the Quality of Educational Experiences Offered to 3- and 4-Year-Olds*, HMSO, 1990

Schools Curriculum and Assessment Authority, *Looking at Children's Learning*, SCAA, HMSO, 1997

Siraj-Blatchford, I., *The Early Years: Laying the Foundation for Racial Equality*, Trentham Books, 1994

Siraj-Blatchford, I. and Siraj-Blatchford, J., *Educating the Whole Child: Cross-Curricular Skills, Themes and Dimensions*, Open University Press

Stoppard, M., *The New Baby Care Book*, Dorling Kindersley, 1990

Wilson, A. and Joseph, Y., *Recognising child abuse: a guide for early years workers*, Starting Points No 6, National Early Years Network, 1990

Premises design

Brown, M., *The Organisation of Space and Resources*, High/Scope, 1990

Matrix and the GLC Women's Committee, *Building for Childcare*, Matrix, 1986 (Note: This guide is available from the Daycare Trust)

National Playing Fields Association, *Technical Advisory Notices*, NPFA (Note: This series of papers includes information about a range of subjects including garden plants, seating, fixed play equipment and gates)

NHS Estates, Design Guide, *The design of day nurseries*, NHS, HMSO, 1991

Ward Lock, *Choosing a Colour Scheme*, Ward Lock, 1997

Health and safety

British Red Cross, *First Aid for Children Fast*, Dorling Kindersley, 1994

Child Accident Prevention Trust, *Accident Prevention in Day Care and Play Settings: A Practical Guide*, CAPT, 1992

Health and Safety Commission, *Management of Health and Safety at Work*, HSE, 1992

Health and Safety Executive, *Essentials of Health and Safety at Work*, HSE, HMSO, 1990

National Early Years Network, *Keeping children healthy: a guide for early years workers*, Starting Points No 8, NEYN, 1991

National Playing Fields Association, *Hard Surfaces for Games and Play Areas*, NPFA, 1989

National Playing Fields Association, *Impact Absorbing Surfaces for Children's Playgrounds*, NPFA, 1997

Nutrition and food

Dare, A. and O'Donovan, M., *A Practical Guide to Child Nutrition*, Stanley Thornes, 1996

Hall, M., *Feeding Your Children*, Piatkus, 1990

Karmel, *The Complete Baby and Toddler Meal Planner*, Edbury Press, 1991

Ministry of Agriculture Fisheries and Food, in Association with DoH and HEA, *Healthy Diets for Infants and Young Children*, MAFF, 1997

Whiting, M. and Lobstein, T., *The Nursery Food Book*, Edward Arnold, 1992

Yntema, S., *Vegetarian Children*, McBooks Press, 1995

Human resources and general management

Adair, J., *Decision Making and Problem Solving*, Institute of Personnel and Development, 1997

Adair, J., *The Action Centred Leader*, The Industrial Society

Advisory Conciliation and Arbitration Service, *Employing People: The ACAS handbook for small firms*, ACAS

Barker, A., *Making Meetings Work*, The Industrial Society

Crosby, P., *Quality is Free*, Penguin

Edwards, L., *Interviewing*, The Industrial Society

Hackett, P., *The Selection Interview*, Institute of Personnel and Development, 1995

Hardingham, A., *Working in Teams*, Institute of Personnel and Development, 1996

Lewis, D., *Essentials of Employment Law*, Institute of Personnel and Development, 1997

McGeough, P., *Team Briefing – A Practical Handbook*, The Industrial Society

Pell, A.R., *The Complete Idiot's Guide to Managing People*, Alpha Books, 1995

Sadgrove, K., *Making TQM Work*, Kogan Page, 1995

Smith, S., *The Quality Revolution*, Management Books 2000 Ltd
Stewart, D.M., *Handbook of Management Skills*, Gower, 1997
Taylor, G., *Equal Opportunities – A Practical Handbook*, The Industrial Society
Walton, P., *Job Sharing: A Practical Guide*, Kogan Page, 1990

Finance and business management

Bennett, R., *How to Set Up and Run Your Own Business*, Kogan Page, 1996
Burns, P. and Dewhurst, J., *Small Business and Entrepreneurship*, Macmillan, 1996
Gardner, D.C., *Introduction to Finance for the Non-Financial Manager*, Pitman, 1996
Gurton, T., *The Penguin Business Directory*, Penguin
National Westminster Bank PLC with the Small Business Centre of Durham University Business School, *The Business Start-Up Guide*, Nat West, 1995
Philip, D.R., *Business Start-Up Checklist*, Accountancy Books ICAEW, 1994
Price, A.St.J., *Understand Your Accounts – A Guide to Small Business Finance*, Kogan Page, 1991
Richardson, P. and Clarke, L., *Business Start-Up for Professional Managers*, Kogan Page, 1993
Williams, D., *Running Your Own Business*, Longman, 1994
Williams, S., *Lloyds Bank Small Business Guide*, Penguin, 1996

Nursery management

Andreski, R. and Nicholls, S., *Managing your nursery*, Nursery World, 1996
Griffin, S., *Keeping and writing records: a step-by-step guide for early years workers*, Starting Points No 17, National Early Years Network, 1994
Hyder, T. and Roels, C., *On Equal Terms: ways to involve parents*, Starting Points No 26, National Early Years Network, 1997
Marsh, L. and Collins, S., *Preparing for early years inspections*, National Early Years Network and the Association of Advisors for Under Eights and Their Families, 1997
Sadek, E. and Sadek, J., *Good Practice in Nursery Management*, Stanley Thornes, 1996

INDEX